Dear George,

I hope you enjoy reading this and adding it to your library.

In friendship

Islamic Activists

The Anti-Enlightenment Democrats

Deina Ali Abdelkader

PlutoPress
www.plutobooks.com

First published 2011 by Pluto Press
345 Archway Road, London N6 5AA and
175 Fifth Avenue, New York, NY 10010

www.plutobooks.com

Distributed in the United States of America exclusively by
Palgrave Macmillan, a division of St. Martin's Press LLC,
175 Fifth Avenue, New York, NY 10010

British Library Cataloguing in Publication Data
A catalogue record for this book is available from the British Library

ISBN   978 0 7453 2217 9   Hardback
ISBN   978 0 7453 2216 2   Paperback

Library of Congress Cataloging in Publication Data applied for

This book is printed on paper suitable for recycling and made from fully managed
and sustained forest sources. Logging, pulping and manufacturing processes are
expected to conform to the environmental standards of the country of origin.

10   9   8   7   6   5   4   3   2   1

Designed and produced for Pluto Press by
Chase Publishing Services Ltd, 33 Livonia Road, Sidmouth, EX10 9JB, England
Typeset from disk by Stanford DTP Services, Northampton, England
Simultaneously printed digitally by CPI Antony Rowe, Chippenham, UK
and Edwards Bros in the USA

*To my parents: Cheridan and Ali Abdelkader,
to Hany, and my one and only Aida*

Contents

Preface   viii

1. Introduction: Orientalism, Islamic Activism
   and Rational Thought?   1
2. The Rudiments of an Islamic Just Society:
   The Contribution of Abu-Ishaq al-Shatibi   29
3. Yusuf al-Qaradawi: Modernization is Key   43
4. Rachid al-Ghannouchi: Minorities and Equality   66
5. Abdessalam Yassine: The Just Ruler   88
6. Conclusion: Reason and Faith: The Islamists
   versus the "Stillborn God"   107

Glossary   126
Notes   132
Bibliography   143
Suggested Reading   150
Index   151

Preface

After teaching about Islamic activism for around ten years, it came to my attention that, although much has been written about the topic since 9/11, we have very few works that address the leaders of populist Islamic movements. A handful of literature addresses their writings but fewer still compare and contextualize these leaders. Because I have been unable to find a book aimed at the general public and students of the Muslim world that transfers this knowledge in a succinct and clear way, I have attempted in this book to fill this gap in the literature.

The objective of this book is twofold: First, to familiarize its audience with popular Islamist leaders, their ideas, and their writings. The three leaders were chosen because they combined "moderate" political activism with ideological activism. Second, to analyze one of the main controversies between Western secular democratic theory and contemporary Islamist writing about governance. The Enlightenment's emphasis on the inevitable conflict between reason and faith underlies the stress on secularism as a prerequisite for democratization. One of the most important components of this book is to compare the Islamists' ideas and how they diverge from the dichotomy between reason and faith that is accepted in Western political thought. This book is designed to fill a gap in the literature on Islam and politics; it should be useful to students and general readers who want to know more about the Middle East as a region and about contemporary Muslim political ideology.

The purpose of this book lies in its attempt to clarify and present a discourse unfamiliar to the Western world, but on its own terms.

Chapter one introduces the reader to the ideological differences that exist between Western liberal thought and Muslim thought. It also clarifies the purpose of the book and its emphasis on Islamic political thought. The second chapter provides an historical example of a Muslim jurist who ties reason to faith. The third, fourth, and fifth chapters discuss and present the lives and ideas of three contemporary Islamists: Qaradawi (a leader of the Muslim Brotherhood of Egypt), Ghannouchi (the leader of the Renaissance Movement in Tunisia), and Yassine (the leader of the Justice and Benevolence Party in Morocco). The final chapter binds the book in a discussion of democracy and whether it is preclusive of faith.

The conclusion therefore ties all the chapters in its pursuit of a definition of democracy or its semblance in the Muslim world.

It is impossible for the breadth of this study to discuss everything that pertains to Islamic governance and therefore women's issues are not presented. The focus of the book is on the general ideological and legal principles that could potentially later be used to decipher the position of women in society and other equally important issues in the details of an Islamic just society. However the rudiments of those details lie in the theoretical analyses and this is where the book's emphasis lies.

The book offers insights into what and how Islamists think about the shape of an ideal government based on their own writing. The uniqueness of this book lies in presenting the Islamists' ideas in their own words to the Western audience. The chapters about Qaradawi, Ghannouchi, and Yassine, enable the reader to experience the Islamists' points of view directly in their own words. A comparison of the roots of democratic ideology with the Islamists' ideal government also sheds light on the semblance of important issues such as the meaning of justice and equality without having to render faith.

I am indebted to Pluto Press for their support and suggestions. I am also hugely indebted to John Voll for his comments when this manuscript was just an idea. My friend and colleague Emad Shahin also guided me along they way. I would also like to thank Mohamad El-Doufani, the BBC editor who edited my work and Roger van Zwanenberg for constantly challenging me and seeing this work through.

I would also like to thank my family for their endless support in this endeavor and the hours they spent on proof-reading the manuscript.

1
Introduction
Orientalism, Islamic Activism
and Rational Thought?

Historical events have regularly shifted the normative bases for the study of Islamic activism. For example, the stance of scholars and the public towards Islamic activism following the 1979 Iranian Revolution was quite different from that during the Afghan resistance to the Russian occupation. The events of September 11, 2001, precipitated yet another tectonic shift in attitudes toward Islamic activism. Once again, public construction of Islamic activism as monolithic—and, in this case, malevolent—challenges any nuanced study of Islamic movements.

Scholars must revitalize research agendas to discern differences among movements and leaders. Furthermore, it is essential to recognize the importance of moderate Islamic activists who are reshaping and redefining certain views and legal precepts in the Islamic faith. The age of scientific revolution in Europe came hand in hand with an assumed supremacy of rational thought. The West equated modernity with all things rational. Hence the divergence in today's world between Islamic thought (contemporary and classical) and the constructs of Western modernity.

For example, Ernest Gellner (1992) writes about being an "Enlightenment Rationalist Fundamentalist" as opposed to an "Islamic Fundamentalist". In his writing, he emphasizes that[1]

> Sociologists have long entertained and frequently endorsed the theory of secularization. It runs as follows: [in] the scientific-industrial society, religious faith and observance decline. One can give intellectualist reasons for this: the doctrines of religion are in conflict with those of science, which in turn are endowed with enormous prestige, and which constitute the basis of modern technology, and thereby also of modern economy. Therefore, religious faith declines. Its prestige goes down as the prestige of its rival rises.
>
> (Gellner 1992: 4)

The binary division between rational versus irrational has continuously represented the strongest point of contention between Western and Islamic thought. The Islamists' call for a return to *sharia* law, or for following the days of *"al-Salaf al-Salih"* (the righteous predecessors) has been assumed to mean a return to a historical golden age, an idea that reeks of romanticism, the arch-opponent of rationalist thought and the very symbol of irrationality.

This binary view of the rational versus the irrational, the Western versus the Islamic, the modern versus the traditional, has led to isolation and detachment in the contemporary analysis of Islamic political movements. However, more importantly—as I am arguing in this book—it has also dismissed the argumentation methods and the use of human reason that Islamic jurisprudential thought has left as a legacy. *Fiqh* is a relevant if not crucial part of contemporary Muslim society whether it is political or apolitical in nature.

Roxanne Euben's *Enemy in the Mirror* critiques the Western theoretical discourse for its total disregard for the relevance of metaphysics in contemporary political life (Euben 1999: 14). Euben states:

For the reflex to dismiss fundamentalism as irrational or pathological is not merely a product of the almost habitualized prejudices and fears operative in the relationship between 'the West' and 'Islam' but, as I have argued, also a function of the way a post-Enlightenment, predominantly rationalist tradition of scholarship countenances foundationalist political practices in the modern world.

(Euben 1999: 14)

Euben's contribution and purpose in her book centers on the argument that fundamentalism is becoming more rather than less powerful, and that those who are worried about the challenge fundamentalists pose to liberal or democratic theory assume that fundamentalism signifies the resurgence of the irrational, the stubborn persistence of archaic and particularistic, or the veil that masks what are essentially structural tensions. Such stories function ultimately to discredit adherents as fanatical lunatics or agents of regressive chaos, or to reduce fundamentalist ideas to mere conduits; they all miss the opportunity to understand the appeals of fundamentalism (Euben 1999: 15).

I would like to take Euben's concerns a step further by arguing that not only is the Enlightenment fixation affecting our understanding of modern Islamic movements and their appeal, but that this fixation is also limiting, if not obliterating, a practical and serious discussion of Islamic legal and political literature.

Euben recounts that the study of Islamic activism is continuously subjugated to an analysis of the Islamic activist's political behavior, while there is a total detachment in this analysis from how the fundamentalists (activists) themselves understand and describe their actions (Euben 1999: 24).

In studying Islamic Activism, one finds there is very little literature that explains the current Islamic discourse on change.

Euben indicates that scholars have intentionally refused to analyze Islamic political theory because of a Western aversion to all things Islamic. This rejection stems from the aversion also to anything religious, as opposed to our contemporary Cartesian Enlightenment "truths". That unwillingness to understand and explain the Islamic vision of the state and Islamic peoples' aspirations for Muslim society has led to the current failure in communication with "the Other".

Thus, every time we are faced with Islamists winning elections in a certain country or with Islamists who get involved in terrorist acts, we have no threshold knowledge to provide us with the analytical and logical tools to comprehend current issues in Muslim societies. The logical question then about Islamic Activism is: If there is change, what will this change entail? As Butterworth notes in his article "Prudence versus Legitimacy" (1982), there are no progressive steps towards an understanding of how social institutions will function beyond rallying popular support, thus indicating the need for a "third wave of thinkers" to address the particular details of justice according to Islamic law (Butterworth 1982: 110).

Butterworth's call for clarity is a concern for a number of researchers on Islamic Activism, for example, Haddad stresses that the challenging task is to understand "change to what?" (Haddad 1991: 7).

Esposito criticizes the Islamic Activists' focus on the failures of the incumbent governments, rather than "defining the nature of an Islamic state and its institutions" (Esposito 1992: 99).

Post September 11, 2001, literature on Islamist ideology is still miniscule. Who are, for example, Qaradawi, Ghannouchi, and Yassine? What are their visions of an Islamic state? These are the questions that this book will answer. It is critical to understand these leaders' aspirations before being able to project and analyze the contemporary Islamists' discourse. This understanding is necessary because it helps differentiate terrorist versus pacifist Islamists and it also sheds light on the kind of debate and rhetoric that even terrorists read and use in our contemporary world. As Haddad, Esposito and others emphasize: Regardless of the Islamic activists differences, all agree on the need to implement Islamic law. However, as Haddad notes (Haddad 1991: 53): "they differ in what they wish to implement. Conservatives tend to regard much of the corpus of the traditional Islamic law as binding. Reformers note that the law is subject to reinterpretation '*al-ijtihad*' and reform."

The works of contemporary Islamic reformists are precisely what this book will address in its effort to analyze and explain their visions and blueprints for an Islamic state.

The assumption that reason and secularism are determinative to an aspiring democracy, in Western liberal thought, necessitates an analysis of the literature. Therefore, the book will analyze whether reason and faith are mutually exclusive in the populist Islamic discourse. The analysis of Islamists writings concerning faith and reason will therefore determine whether secularism is a prerequisite for establishing a democracy.

OLD CONSTRUCTS IN A NEW WORLD

In the midst of the Iranian Revolution and the hostage crisis, Western publics, the Western media, and even some scholars saw Islamic activists as violent, unreasoning enemies. Whether such blanket vilification was morally acceptable is not the concern of this study. More significant for subsequent events was the dehumanization of activist Iranians that blinded the West to the populist aspect of the revolution. This inability to understand the populist element underlying the events in Iran led to the West's incomprehension as to the motives behind the September 11, 2001, attacks and subsequent public demonstrations of seemingly murderous satisfaction in the East. Al-Qaeda and its leaders do not represent populist Islamic movements. However, the political powerlessness of moderate Islamists has enabled the influence of violent Islamic groups to grow.

Cold War paradigms of confrontation were useless to US leaders in meeting the challenge of violent Islamic groups. The bipolarity of the international system dominating the post-war period was based on shifting alliances that gave some nations with little power of their own (such as Egypt and Indonesia) disproportionate political roles in international relations. With the disintegration of the Warsaw Pact and consolidation of the US as the unopposed global hegemon, less powerful nations have fewer opportunities to form alliances that will improve their fortunes and influence. The frustration engendered by a hegemonic power impervious to the influence of other nations provides a rich medium for the growth of Islamic activism.

The Cold War paradigm recognized modern nation states as the sole actors on the international stage. But in the last 20 years, ethnic and religious cleavages have challenged the internal cohesion of nation-states. Stateless, often transboundary nations, have asserted their rights and identities; non-state actors, such as Osama bin Laden and Al-Qaeda, have become game-changing players in Afghanistan and Saudi Arabia. Both trends have led to severe rifts in the composition of nation-states that previously characterized twentieth century, particularly post-World War Two, politics.

From this perspective, the US bombing of Afghanistan had minimal impact on "the enemy"—very different from what it might have had in a Cold War scenario. Also, in requesting that Saudi Arabia change its religious education curricula, US leaders were seen to be arrogantly dictating to a sovereign state. Such high-handed tactics diminish the advance of Western interests in the Muslim world. More dangerously, the alienation of Saudi Arabians plays right into the hands of Bin Laden and his like.

Clearly, a foreign policy that relies on archaic Cold War analyses is inadequate to current challenges. To comprehend the dynamics of Islamic populist movements and the new international landscape of players and actors, the contemporary international political milieu needs to make an analytical, if not a paradigmatic, shift..

This study is designed to reconstruct this landscape to include the voices of several populist Islamic leaders. The clarification of their positions and motives offers important insights into critical social and political issues in the confrontation between Islamists and the West.

First and foremost, it is necessary to clarify and define what I mean by "populist Islamists". In the roughly two decades between the 1979 Iranian revolution and September 11, 2001, political perception of Islamic activists[2] shifted and changed. The revolution and subsequent seizure of US hostages in Tehran cast political Islam in a very negative light among Western media commentators, politicians, and even academics. The Russian invasion of Afghanistan shifted the normative view toward a conception favoring the "mujahideen" and their efforts against Russian forces. In this way, political events and alliances forced and informed perceptions of Islamists in popular culture, foreign relations, teaching, and research relating to Islamic movements.

During this period, terms such as the "green peril", "clash of civilizations", and the historical view that "Islam has bloody borders" (Huntington 1993: 34-35) became common in the literature on political Islam, activist movements, and their leaders. The events of 9/11 reinforced these trends in discussions of Islamic politics. Only a handful of scholars have been able to set aside those images and see the legitimacy and appeal of these groups to their fellow co-nationalists within their own civil societies.

Ten years later, there are still very few scholars who can see populist Islam as an expression of legitimate civil concerns. Populist Islamists are Islamic political leaders who are engaged in a dialogue with their respective societies. Their representations of the ideal political and social ethos are legitimate in the eyes of their constituents. In their writing and other political expression, populist Islamists are largely interpreters of civil grievances and definers of ideal governance.

Populist Islamists had long been active in the region. Hassan al-Banna's Muslim Brotherhood, founded in 1928, grew rapidly in the Middle East, soon transcending its boundaries as far as Pakistan and Indonesia. This movement attracted attention when it began to mobilise the population against British rule. Recruitment of Muslim Brothers was fueled largely by resistance to the British occupation of Egypt at the time. This anti-colonialist movement inspired other political nationalist forces against foreign occupation. It is my goal in this book therefore to focus on Islamists who have a foot in both realms: The political (practical) as well as theoretical (ideological) realm.

I have selected Qaradawi as a contemporary ideological leader of the Muslim Brothers, the first Islamic politically active group in the Middle East (established in 1928). The second activist is Ghannouchi of Tunisia because both Qaradawi and Ghannouchi are intellectuals who have participated in organized political activism and they both have engaged in creating and sharing with the masses their view of an "ideal" Islamic state. My third example of Islamic activist writing is Yassine of Morocco who, like Qaradawi and Ghannouchi, is simultaneously a prolific author and an activist.

A second reason for choosing these three Islamists is their popularity amongst the masses in their respective societies as well as their knowledge and ability to conduct their political discourse in a "moderate" spirit. That is to say, they all engage in deciphering Islamic mores and canons from a liberal/moderate[3] perspective, following human reasoning when applicable like a historial figure called Shatibi that I mention later in this book.

A third reason is a logistical one in that, like many other researchers, the availability and accessibility of the works of these Islamists facilitated my selection in terms of finding appropriate materials upon which to conduct and base my research.

Very few studies elaborate on contemporary political Islamists; those that do include AzzamTamimi (2001), John Esposito and John Voll (2001), Hakan Yavuz (2003) and Noah Feldman (2004, 2008). Of these, an even smaller group of scholars focuses on those Islamic activists who bridge the political/practice arena and the scholar/ideologue realm. Research on Muslim intellectuals has focused on thinkers such as Hassan Hanafi and Mohammed Emara, who are not practicing politicians. Analyses of Islamic activist leaders involved in both theory and practice realms are still marginal and rare.

One important reason for this unbalanced view is, as indicated earlier, the dominant influence of realpolitik on public and academic perceptions of Islamic activists. Fawaz Gerges's *America and Political Islam: Clash of Cultures or Clash of Interests* (Gerges 1999) provides a detailed analysis of this problem. Another reason that moderate Islamic activists have not been widely included in the discourse on comparative democracy and political theory is that two powerful forces contend against thorough investigation of Islamic activism research.

First, the relationship of a hegemon to satellite countries exemplifies the Foucaultian notion that knowledge is tied to power.[4] If we accept this, "knowledge" is subservient to maintaining the status quo. Thus, the control of defining knowledge and its components is ultimately held by the hegemon. As Bernard Lewis comments in *What Went Wrong?* (2002): "Today, for the time being, as Ataturk recognized and as Indian computer scientists and Japanese high-tech companies appreciate the dominant civilization is Western, and Western standards therefore define modernity" (Lewis 2002: 150).

Second, any writings on moderate Islamists must contend with the hard line drawn during the Enlightenment between faith and reason. This idea, embedded in Western thought, deeply affects perceptions of Islamic activism. The research agendas of scholars writing on the topic are inevitably shaped by this accepted polarity. Gellner, for example, presents himself as an "Enlightenment Rationalist Fundamentalist" as opposed to an Islamic Fundamentalist.

The radical discontinuity between faith and reason, essential to the Enlightenment project, lies at the heart of the Muslim/Western discourse. Disagreement over the nature of democratic practices, modernization, or egalitarian reform all stem from different perceptions of the relationship—or lack thereof—between faith and reason.

THE ENLIGHTENMENT, RATIONALITY AND THEIR DISCONTENTS

First, let me clarify the link between the incumbent discourse on Islamic activism, and the "Enlightenment", the harbinger of modernization. The seeming contradiction between reason and faith stems from our contemporary understanding of the relation between the precepts of modernity/democratization and the Enlightenment notion of reason or the "rational".

The invocation of the use of reason, as explained by the German philosopher Immanuel Kant, distinguishes using rasonieren in public versus private arenas. He says that in public rasonieren should be used liberally. However, reason in the private sphere should play a secondary role. The word rasonieren, in German, as noted by Foucault: "[D]oes not refer to just any use of reason, but to a use of reason in which reason has no other end but itself: rasonieren is to reason for reasoning's sake" (Foucault 1984: 36).

European circumstances in Kant's time influenced his view of rasonieren. Until the eighteenth century nothing united Western culture as strongly and powerfully as the Christian faith. No matter what one's social status, serf or king, one's first allegiance was unquestionably to the Christian Church. While challenges to Church authority occurred prior to the Enlightenment era, none were so rigorous and united in destabilizing the Church's position as the Enlightenment movement.

The German philosopher Kant (1724-1804) was one of the moderate Enlightenment thinkers: He believed in God's existence. However he challenged the monopoly of schools, churches, and universities in defining reason. Other strands of Enlightenment thought included the deists who called for the severance of human concerns and life from all things divine. Another group, known as pantheists or materialists (labeled by their opponents as atheists) deified Nature and proposed the elimination of all other forms of worship and divinity.

French skeptics laid the cornerstone of modern "rational" thought. Philosophers such as Descartes, Pierre Bayle (Bayle 1740) and Voltaire,[5] challenged the monopoly of religious and social hierarchies over "truth". Groups such as the English Freethinkers and Freemasons who espoused similar views emerged in other parts of Europe in the late seventeenth and early eighteenth centuries. This age also saw the stirrings of a revolution in scientific thought, in which the study of natural processes began to differentiate the natural from the supernatural.

In this period, a wide range of ideas that came together in Enlightenment philosophy shared a commitment to demolishing Church authority and questioning all the ideas it engendered or claimed. This duality and antagonism created the rift that we see today between reason and faith. The suspicion and fear of religion and the Church institution-alized in the age of Enlightenment continues to influence and inform the social sciences including subfields such as political sociology, comparative politics, and political theory. The relation between contemporary political theory and the Enlightenment, and between contemporary political theory and Islamic activism, will be elaborated later in this chapter.

In reaction to the Enlightenment, there was a rise of what is termed "irrational" thought in Europe. The backlash against rationalism has important implications about the growing divide between faith and reason, the rational versus the irrational. The rejection of scientific/rational thought in Europe may be traced back to the consequent loss of spirituality and the breakdown of Christian traditions and mores on which people relied.

"Irrationalism" focused on human nature, on man's drives and impulses, as opposed to the valorization of man's intellect proposed by the "rationalist" school. Important Irrationalist philosophers included Schopenhauer and later Nietzsche. The ideas of Henri Bergson, George Sorel, and Sigmund Freud are also examples of the "irrational" school in the late 1800s.

Nietzsche's writing about Europe's need for an egalitarian "superman" or "overman", was used by the Nazis to legitimize the persecution of groups that failed to meet an imagined "Aryan" ideal. Even though Nietzsche was an ardent Church critic (unlike Bergson), his break with "rational" thought intensified the philosophical divide between the rational versus the irrational.

European/Western historical memory includes two critical junctures at which rejection of the "rational" retarded science and threatened moral values. Whether we analyze medieval Catholic control and dictatorship in the West or the horrors of Nazi Germany, the Western psyche was rightfully doubtful and troubled by any movement or idea that transcended the so-called "rational" realm.

Enlightenment Europe embraced scientific advances that translated into new forms of human productivity, including colonialism. Entrepreneurs sought raw materials and markets in newly-accessible lands. Social scientists and popular writers applied the insights of such heroes of rationalism as Charles Darwin and Herbert Spencer to legitimize occupations and colonizations beyond Europe, including those of Muslim countries.

COLONIALISM AND ITS DISCONTENTS

Colonialism arose in the wake of the Enlightenment. The colonial era started with the Napoleonic invasion of Egypt in 1798. Thierry Hentsch (1992) describes: "The marriage of Enlightenment and Imperialism wherein the husband never failed to subjugate the lovely wife to his basest designs" (Hentsch 1992: 122).

Nineteenth century research relating to Muslim countries, based on rational and scientific principles, bolstered the sense that the Occident was becoming more knowledgeable about the Orient than the Orient itself: "England knows Egypt; Egypt is what England knows; England knows that Egypt cannot have self-government; England confirms that by occupying Egypt" (Hentsch 1992: 155). Knowledge and curiosity about the Muslim "Other" became a cultural norm.

This sense of self confidence preceded and justified colonization. During the seventeenth and early part of the eighteenth century, Europe viewed the Ottoman Empire as a powerful peer. However, the growing economic weakness of the Ottomans led to the loss of power over their territories at a time that Europe was gaining wealth and colonized territory. The crumbling of the Ottoman Empire by association diminished their faith, Islam, in Western eyes. The ideological, social, and political void left by the destabilized Ottomans was soon filled with Western interests: "From this moment onward, our image of the Other was shaped neither by curiosity nor by the presumptuous desire to transform, but, in the rawest terms, by the European's power to dominate and to exploit" (Hentsch 1992: 130).

It is really with Hegelian thought that the juncture between Enlightenment "reason" and the justification for colonialism became apparent. Hegel writes:

> The Orientals do not know that the spirit or man as such are free in themselves ... Only the Germanic nations, with the rise of Christianity, were the first to realize that man is by nature free, and that freedom of the spirit is his very essence.
>
> (Hegel 1975 edition: 54)

Hegel attributed the European march of history to the dynamism of religion: "History merely revealed the eternal immanence of Reason in the universe. So it came to pass that Europe regulated the world, and in the mouth of Hegel, revealed the meaning of history: Reason, in other words God, had spoken" (Hentsch 1992: 141).

The imagery of Muslim women in pre-colonial and colonial times reinforces the stark divisions perceived to lie between the civilized and the uncivilized worlds, between societies that adhere to reason/science versus the Other that adheres to religious/irrational modes of thought:[6] "I willingly parted with a few paras for the purpose of establishing an intercourse with fellow-creatures so fearfully and wonderfully resembling the tailless baboon" (Sir Richard Burton, *Personal Narrative of a Pilgrimage to Al-Madinah and Meccah*, 1907, Vol. I, 406–7).

An earlier commentator asserted that:

An Eastern lady is the most uncouth and inelegant form imaginable. On foot, too, her appearance is not much improved; for the awkward boots and slippers compel her to slide and roll along in such an ungainly manner as forcibly to remind the beholder of a duck waddling to a pond, or of a bundle of clothes on short thick stilts. To complete the picture, it must be left to those European ladies who have had the fortune to gain admission to the privacy of a harem, to state whether the tone and conversation of their Mohammedan friends is more polished and elegant than their external appearance; many a fair form is concealed beneath a rough exterior; but, if we may judge of the fair sex of Islam by the native Christian ladies, I fear the answer will not be satisfactory."

(William Kennett Loftus, *Travels and Researches in Chaldea and Susiana*, 1857, 68–9)

The dehumanization of Muslim women as baboons legitimizes the conquest and rule of such "fearful creatures". Travel and scientific literature was rife with examples justifying the "White Man's Burden", the responsibility of the West to civilize the East:

Easily could one pick out among the number those who had received advantage of some education under European training. Their figures were disciplined, they held themselves erect, and sat on chairs or stools. Their expression had depth. Faculties of observation and disposition, still latent in others, manifested by the dumb wistfulness of many a dark eye, had been called into action.

(A.C. Inchbold, *Under the Syrian Sun*, 1906: vol. II, 416–17)[7]

This attitude, generally known as "Orientalism", may be identified in the writing of Chateaubriand as well as Edward Lane and Lamartine (Said 1978: 179). The late Edward

Said's arguments in *Orientalism* (1978) are later expanded in *Culture and Imperialism* (1993).

The present study owes much to the work of Hentsch and Said. However, I differ with their fundamental contention that the totality of Western understanding of Muslim societies is based on and limited only to power relationships. In fact, some contemporaries of Chateaubriand, Lane, and Lamartine, such as Louis Massignon and Jacques Berque critically rejected their views.

Their voices were drowned out by the wave of popular and scientific consensus that reinforced the dualistic analysis of civilized versus uncivilized. Even though there was no uniform continuum of "Orientalism" as depicted by Said; there was definitely a continuum of binary divisions between "Us" (the civilized) and "Them" (the uncivilized). This idea was articulated in new forms by writers who accepted the Weberian vision of the relationship between religion and society.

RATIONALISM, WEBER AND MODERN ISLAMIC ACTIVISM

The stress on rational versus irrational continued to develop in Europe in the social science field. Max Weber's influential work *The Protestant Ethic and the Spirit of Capitalism* (1904), deepened the rift seen by social scientists between traditional and modern societies. Weber saw rationality as a precondition to modernization. As Davis[8] explains, Weber studied development as a unilateral obstacle course the successful negotiation of which converts traditional societies (who depend on "irrational" forms of traditional social organization such as family and tribal ties) into modern societies. Modern societies, according to Weber, were not only able to let go of traditional social structures, but were also able to institutionalize rationality in the form of bureaucracies.

Thus another qualification that irrational, traditional societies must meet to become rationally modern found its way into Western thought. This division continues and is echoed in contemporary times in characterizing democratic versus undemocratic practices, and qualifying modern versus traditional societies.

How does this binary division influence the study of Islamic activism, its leaders, and Muslim societies in general? Contemporary social scientists such as Deeb (1992) and Dekmejian (1985) link traditionalism and charismatic authority to current Islamic movements and their leaders. Studies that take such an approach link traditional types of action to Islamic activism. For example, Burke writes: "Until the last few decades, the great majority of social movements in Islamic societies tended to be situated within the Weberian tradition, though often without much methodological self-awareness" (Burke and Lapidus 1988: 20)

Another offshoot of the "Weberian" analysis of Islamic activism is separating the rational from the irrational as illustrated by Kenz (1991: 104):

One then proceeds to a classification of social ideologies according to the dyad religious base/rational base which are distributed among the various actor categories. Two well-formed classes sufficiently powerful and homogenous will correspond to ideologies whose rational elements dominate; to the unstable, precarious, distorted classes will correspond those where the irrational element, particularly religion, will dominate.

In *Egypt Under Nasser* (1971), Dekmejian's stretched the Weberian paradigm, using "what Weber calls charismatic authority" to analyze Gamal Abdel-Nasser's rule. Dekmejian also observes that it is hard to conceptualize charisma because of the "inability of democratic man to conceptualize such a foreign experience" (Dekmejian 1971: 3). Pursuing this theme in Islam and Revolution, Dekmejian explains Islamic movements: "The ideologies of these movements are both comprehensive and rigid, reflecting the responses of typically charismatic leaders to situations of crisis. The Islamist movements of the present are no exception" (Dekmejian 1985: 25). From this perspective, he sees similarities between Nasser's Egypt and current Islamic activists in several Middle Eastern countries.

However, this position runs the risk of oversimplifying the Weberian paradigm. His argument (about two separate political phenomena in Egypt) states that any popular movement is a result of charismatic leadership. He discounts the fact that although most movements have their heroes, the appeal of the leader is only a partial and superficial explanation for the success of the movement. This argument implies that the dynamic of grassroots movements is directly related to the irrational processes of a society that runs contradictory to rationality and its practice as embodied in "legal-rational" institutions, democracy, and the values of liberalism.

Enlightenment duality and the Weberian paradigm, long influential in studying Islamic activism, remain widespread. For example, see Ernest Gellner:

[W]hen dealing with serious matters, when human lives and welfare are at stake, when major resources are being committed, the only kind of knowledge which may legitimately be used and invoked is that which satisfies the criteria of Enlightenment philosophy.

(Gellner 1992: 92)

Gellner writes:

> [The Enlightenment Philosophy] strove to understand the economic
> and social success of the first modern societies, and so proposed
> a secular version of a salvation religion, a naturalistic doctrine of
> universally valid salvation, in which reason and nature replaced
> revelation. It did so because it perceived the role of new secular
> knowledge in the new social order.
>
> (Gellner 1992: 90)

Gellner claims that the "cognitive ethic" of the Enlightenment
treats: "all data, all information, all occasions, alike: there
are no privileged sources of illumination. The essence of sin
is the making of exceptions. In other words, there is no and
can be no revelation" (Gellner 1992: 83–4).

He vehemently believes that, like himself, all sociologists
endorse the theory of secularization, which he views as being
in total opposition to religion. For Gellner, there are no shades
of grey: either modernity-secularism or religion can be a guide
to social behavior. Only when one is in decline will the other
rise in importance and authority (Gellner 1992: 4).

As mentioned earlier, the relation between contemporary
political theory, the Enlightenment, and how Islamic activists
and their writings are perceived in the literature has been
competently discussed by Roxanne Euben in *Enemy in
the Mirror* (1999). She argues that "political theory is an
enterprise perhaps produced by, but not coterminous with,
Western civilization" (Euben 1999: 10). Euben explains that:

> [T]he reflex to dismiss fundamentalism as irrational or pathological
> is not merely a product of the almost habitualized prejudices and
> fears operative in the relationship between 'the West' and 'Islam' but,
> as I have argued, also a function of the way a post-Enlightenment,

predominantly rationalist tradition of scholarship countenances a foundationalist political practice in the modern world.

(Euben 1999: 14)

Euben is skeptical of any "universal truth" whether it is religious or rationalist, believing that the Enlightenment/ rationalist discourse proselytizes just as much as any religious fundamentalism. She characterizes "rationalist truths" as being "dismissive of other points of view as wrong and dangerous". Euben's most important contribution is her analysis of how current Islamic activists are viewed in comparative political theory:

> The study of modern Islamic fundamentalism is thus often reduced to an examination of fundamentalist political behavior divorced from fundamentalists' own understandings of action: Ideology is understood as the set of beliefs that at once obscures and expresses what essentially structural tensions are. The subtext of this reading is that the growing appeal of fundamentalism owes little to its own inherent power as a moral ideal. As Foucault has pointed out, to be irrelevant is to be shut out of the realm of what is normal and acceptable; it is to be silenced as if mad.
>
> (Euben 1999: 24)

STRUCTURAL FUNCTIONALISTS AND ISLAMIC ACTIVISM

Another genre of analysis also accompanied the Weberian analysis of Islamic movements and Muslim societies, namely "Structural Functionalism".

"Structural functionalists" were theorists who followed the Weberian paradigm. However, they added new dimensions to what they viewed as the necessary steps to modernization.

They focused on issues such as "continuity", "evolutionary change", and the ability of the political system to absorb change (Almond 1982, Apter 1965, Binder 1971, Parsons 1977). As a corollary to the Weberian concept of a "legal-rational authority", they stressed institutionalization as a prerequisite for modernity.

Following the Second World War and the rise of the USSR and the US as superpowers, the debate about modernity was influenced by the ideologies of the two political camps. Along with the creation of NATO and the implementation of the Marshall Plan, the political/social theories offered for development/modernity were subsequently dominated by the ideological bipolarity of the international system.

Post-World War Two views on modernity primarily focused on the predominantly secular elite in the Middle East: the young nationalists of the newly-created Middle Eastern states. Over time, however, the Islamists, who had been part of several national struggles for independence in the region, began to reappear on the political scene, stimulating a new direction in the literature on modernity.

Toward the end of the 1970s, especially after the Iranian revolution in 1979 and the assassination of Egyptian President Anwar Sadat in 1981, attention became focused on the rise of Islamic activism. One causal explanation that has persisted for 30 years is that these societies are reacting to the advent of "modernity". Piscatori's work, for example, illustrates this assumption of a causal relationship:

> [T]he process of development has been a contributing factor. It has stimulated the revival in two main ways: 1) it has often strained the social and political fabric, thereby leading people to turn to traditional symbols and rites as a way of comforting and orienting themselves,

and 2) it has provided the means of speedy communication and easy dissemination of both domestic and international information.

(Piscatori 1986: 27)

Several scholars have looked for a link between Islamic activism and modernity. Vatikiotis explains that the Islamic resurgence is caused by "disaffection" with the changes imposed on these societies by the advent of modernity (Vatikiotis 1981: 193). The disaffection to which Vatikiotis and others refer is summed up in a comment by Gilles Kepel about Islamic movements: "Education has taught them [Islamists] the mannerisms of modern life but not its techniques and spirit" (Kepel 1985: 235).

All these perspectives share the common supposition that these Islamic movements are by-products of a universal "crisis of modernity". By defining Islamic activism as a product or reaction, the analyst implicitly judges these movements as adverse and inimical reactions to modernization and development. By assuming that Islamic activism is caused by discomfort with modernization, these explanations also assume that the movements and their leaders are at odds with modernization and development.

In these writings the link between Islamic activism and modernity is vague, because modernity is not a universal concept. Foucault writes that modernity is an attitude.[9] If so, an assumption that rapid change, development, and modernization are causal factors is theoretically dubious, since there is no clear conception of a unilateral schema of modernization/development. In this view, Islamic activism is perceived to be a regressive force even though there are no clear definitions or empirical studies that specify what constitutes "modernization". Despite numerous studies on the stagnation of development in the Middle East and other Muslim regions, Islamic activism is explained as a phenomenon resisting change and development.

Islamic activism is not the only phenomenon explained away by the so-called "crisis of modernity". Religious differences are also linked to the perceived threat to Western "modernity" from Islamic civilization. Lewis writes:

> We are facing a mood and a movement far transcending the level of issues and politics and the governments that pursue them. This is no less than a clash of civilizations—the perhaps irrational but surely historic reaction of an ancient rival against our Judeo-Christian heritage, our secular present, and the world-wide expansion of both.
>
> (Lewis 1990: 60)

Huntington concurs:

> In Eurasia the great historic fault lines between civilizations are once more aflame. This is particularly true along the boundaries of the crescent-shaped Islamic bloc of nations from the bulge of Africa to central Asia. Violence also occurs between Muslims, on the one hand, and Orthodox Serbs in the Balkans, Jews in Israel, Hindus in India, Buddhists in Burma and Catholics in the Philippines. Islam has bloody borders.
>
> (Huntington 1993: 34–5)

Another assumption is that Western style democracy is a component of modernity. Miller claims that Arabs and Muslims could never value or commit to democracy and justice because historically Arabs and Muslims were never ruled democratically (Miller 1993: 46).

Another example of tying faith to democracy is found in Huntington:

A strong correlation exists between Western Christianity and democracy. Modern democracy developed first and most vigorously in Christian countries ... Democracy was especially scarce among countries that were predominantly Muslim, Buddhist, or Confucian. This correlation does not prove causation. Western Christianity emphasizes, however, the dignity of the individual and the separate spheres of church and state. In many countries, Protestant and Catholic leaders have been central in the struggles against repressive countries. It seems plausible to hypothesize that the expansion of Christianity encourages democratic development.

(Huntington 1991: 72–3)

In addition to the aforementioned criteria for measuring "development/modernity" in Muslim societies, the question of women in Islam has also been used as a yardstick to measure a society's degree of development:

The way Arab women dressed was the most often used sign of progress—that is, Westernization or lack of it. Anonymous women were those who were not Westernized in dress; on the other hand, a miniskirt apparently gave a woman an identity and a university education. A 1979 article on Bahrain charted what the author called 'feminine progress' in three generations of women sighted in the gold bazaar: Grandma moved like a shadow under layers of black ... Mother wore the same black aba, or cloak, but with exposed face and hands ... The youngest, in her teens, sported a fashionable red pantsuit. A red pantsuit signified feminine progress when compared to the veil. Readers need not know anything more about an Arab woman than that she wore a pantsuit or a veil; dress said it all.

(Steet 2000: 133)

The women interviewed by Elizabeth Fernea for her documentary entitled *A Veiled Revolution* seemed to be actively and non-submissively choosing to veil. As Nilufer Gole notes: "The question of women lies at the center of the modernization mentality, which favored the Western notion of universality in opposition to tradition, and particularly, Islam" (Gole 1996: 29).

CONCLUSION

This progression, through the Enlightenment writers, colonial perceptions, the Weberian paradigm, structural-functionalists/ modernization theory, and the current analysis of Islamic movements and their leaders, all represents a continuum of binary divisions. These divisions were and still are the products of historical circumstance and the cultural memory of the West. The understanding of rationality, modernity, and democratic practice has also been built on the historical/ cultural memories of the Western experience.

Unfortunately, the majority of studies of Islamic activism and its leaders fall into two analytical traps: Some investigators have chosen to study Islamic movements as a temporary malaise or a hindrance to proper development and civility. This genre perpetuates the division between "Us" (the civilized, modern, and democratic) and "Them" (the uncivilized, backward, and undemocratic). The second group is the "cultural relativist" genre, in which Islamic movements, for example, are considered rationalist because in the end they achieve their prioritized goals. These writers try to include Islamic movements in their analysis but still cling to assumptions leading to the externalization of Islamic movements and their leaders. Both sets of analysts highlight profound differences.

This chapter illustrates that the influence of the Enlightenment era is still alive and well in political theory as applied to Islamic activist movements. Said would argue that the historical continuum does represent an "Orientalist" bias. The continuum presented in this chapter reveals at different points across time that there are specific binary divisions between the rational and the irrational and primarily between reason and faith. The trajectory of history reflects ebbs and flows in the Western perception of Muslim societies and Islamic movements. Over time, these perceptions were not consistently negative, and not all purposefully designed to serve relations of power and realpolitik, although in certain periods, for example in pre-colonial and colonial times, they did abet power and realpolitik interests.

One could argue that contemporary analyses of Islamic movements reflect realpolitik interests and biases. However, as in Lamartine and Berque's day, two opposing schools of thought, Lewis and Huntington versus Esposito and Voll, are in contention. The paradigmatic and epistemological influences of the Enlightenment are alive and well in contemporary research agendas.

It is only through constructive comparisons and analyses of compatible ideas/practices that the conceptual division between rational/irrational, modern/traditional, democratic/ undemocratic will be laid to rest at last. Such comparisons can only begin through an understanding of the leaders/ ideologues of Islamic movements both on their own merits and in a comparative framework. As Euben writes:

> In part, then, current scholarship on fundamentalism is an exercise in power: the power to construct and control a subject that has little opportunity to contest either the interpretation or the terms of the discourse; the power to dictate the parameters of the field, from which experts regularly pronounce the identity, meaning, and function of a

movement without reference to the adherents' own understanding
of the connection between action and meaning.

(Euben 1999: 43)

This book is an effort to provide contemporary Islamic
leaders with the control and the capacity to define their own
discourse. Once this is achieved, scholars and activists can
embark upon a constructive comparison between Western
political thought and Muslim political thought. The objective
is to build an intellectual space in which the work of Islamic
movement leaders may be examined in terms of their own
reasoning and how it relates to their actions.

First and foremost, it is important to distinguish and
clarify the historical roots of contemporary Islamic writings.
The Islamic writers/activists discussed here, all relate their
ideas to Islamic rules and mores combined with human
reasoning. Their ability to combine the textual sources with
human reasoning is not of their exclusive creation. Islamic
law and its interpretation has depended solely on the works
of jurisprudential thinkers from the rise of Islam until
contemporary times.

The engagement of human reasoning and its importance
has been stressed since the faith's inception, one historical
figure elaborated on its importance and necessity in Islamic
jurisprudence: Shatibi (who lived in Southern Spain in
the 1300s). Shatibi's important contributions have largely
influenced contemporary Islamic thought.

2

The Rudiments of an Islamic Just Society: The Contribution of Abu-Ishaq al-Shatibi

THE IMPORTANCE OF ISLAMIC LAW (*SHARIA*) AND JURISPRUDENCE (*FIQH*) IN THE ISLAMIC POLITICAL DISCOURSE

Firstly, it has to be noted that *al-sharia* is recognized by all Muslims as the set of rules and mores decreed by the Qur'an and the Prophet's tradition (*sunna*: his sayings and actions). Even though some Muslims might argue for secularism and a separation between religion and the state, they would still recognize *al-sharia* as an embodiment of Islamic codes and regulations.

In describing the importance of *sharia* to Muslim society, Charnay notes:

> In Islam the law aims at providing guidance; but not as a mere instrument. It has a much more far-reaching vocation. It creates a model of living and tends to regulate all human activity, or to qualify it with respect, if not to an ethics, at least to a law, transcending not only the individual, but all humanity. Furthermore, Muslim law is not only pragmatic. Over and above the striving for efficaciousness and security, it constitutes an act of piety in its application. The general rule is absolute for the believer, who however modest

his condition, must respect it. It is a blessing to strive continually for a better attainment of that end. In view of this moral purpose, the social desiderata of non-contradiction and legal efficaciousness shrink in importance.

(Charnay 1971: 77–8)

Schact also describes the place of *sharia* and *fiqh* in Muslim societies:

Islamic law is the epitome of Islamic thought, the most typical manifestation of the Islamic way of life, the core and kernel of Islam itself. The very term *al-fiqh*, knowledge, shows that early Islam regarded knowledge of the sacred law as the knowledge par excellence ... But even at the present time the Law, including its legal subject matter, it remains an important, if not the most important, element in the struggle which is being fought in Islam between traditionalism and modernism under the impact of Western ideas. Apart from this, the whole life of the Muslims, Arabic literature, and the Arabic and Islamic disciplines of learning are deeply imbued with the ideas of Islamic law; it is impossible to understand Islam without understanding Islamic law.

(Schact 1964: 1)

In agreement with Schact, on the role of *sharia* in prevailing discussions in Muslim countries, Noori emphasizes:

The ongoing discussion is now centered upon the type of approach to Islamic law which should be adopted by modern Islamic legislators and jurists who are required to find solutions to the problems facing modern Muslim societies by digging into the corpus of the classic works produced by jurists of the medieval time. This is the greatest challenge which faces the advocates of law reform on the one hand and the campaigners for the purification and decolonization of law in Muslim countries on the other. They have to define their own relationship vis-à-vis the great masters of Islamic jurisprudence whose

Institutional Writings have been accepted in respective schools of
Islamic law without questioning for generations.

(Noori 1987: 25)

Thus, *sharia* and *fiqh* are held by a number of Muslim
scholars to be a "pure" form of Muslim thought. Fasi, for
example, maintains that even though Roman, Greek, Persian
and Indian civilizations have affected Muslim culture in many
ways, legal theory (*fiqh*) has retained its uniqueness (al-Fasi
1972: 94–5). Therefore, according to al-Fasi, in order to
restructure Muslim thought and utilize *sharia* in Muslim
courts of law, the study of *fiqh*, its sources and end-goals, is
an indispensable necessity (al-Fasi 1972: 95).

Manzoor links *al-sharia* with the socio-political order:

Any revival of Islamic thought, it goes without saying, is contingent
upon the Muslim effort to revive the methodological framework of
the *sharia*. Only a creative reinterpretation of the *sharia's* legacy that
enables it to work under modern conditions and yet be in consonance
with the Islamic conscience, would lend meaning and cogency to the
moral and civilizational aspirations of Muslims today. For submerged
beneath all the cross-currents of political activism and resurgence lies
the bedrock of Islamic conscience that serves as the moral foundation
of the Muslim's historical search for justice and equity.

(Manzoor 1988: 1)

Again, in stressing *sharia's* role in society, Esposito reminds
us: "Islamic law has remained central to Muslim identity
and practice, for it constitutes the ideal social blueprint for
the good society. The *sharia* has been a source of law and
moral guidance, the basis for both law and ethics" (Esposito
1988: 75).

Modern and contemporary Islamic ideologues have also stressed the importance of *sharia* and *fiqh*. For example, Qutb writes of the importance of *fiqh* as the "theoretical space allowing for change", however, this is expected to be within the constraints of the general framework of *sharia*. According to Qutb, *sharia* is a constant body of rules that do not change since they dictate God's word, derived from the Qu'ran and *sunna*. *Fiqh*, however, is promulgated by people, which makes it more flexible and inclusive of the changes and needs that take place in society (Qutb 1988: 50).

Al-Turabi (1980), one of the recognized Islamic leaders in Sudan, as well as Ghannouchi (Darwish 1992) of *al-Nahda* (the popular Islamic party in Tunisia) have both stressed the importance of *sharia* to the Muslim state. They have also stressed the importance of returning to *fiqh* as a guide for extrapolating a futuristic vision of Muslim society.

SHATIBI'S SIGNIFICANCE IN ISLAMIC JURISPRUDENCE

Shatibi's Life and the Socio-Political Environment of His Age

Shatibi is a well recognized Muslim jurisconsult (*faqih*), he lived most of his life and got most of his education in Granada, Spain. His date of birth is not known, but he died in 1388. Shatibi lived in an age of political turmoil for two reasons: Firstly, Muslims were losing power in Andalusia, and secondly, there was a fierce power struggle going on in Granada, and more specifically, the city of Jativa (where Shatibi gets his name) had signed an agreement with King James stating that Jativa should become semi-sovereign under its Muslim leader. Along with this unrest came the instability of political life, even though the advent of people from Andalusia created a thought-provoking milieu. The Andalusians who fled to Granada at the time were said to have the best clothes and the women were well adorned with jewelry.

The advent of the Andalusians to Granada transferred to them knowledge about farming and small-scale industry. The Andalusians were also very fond of singing, so that Granadans noted that Andalusians sang in public even in the market.

Both Andalusians and North Africans traveled to Granada at this time, and this definitely led to a lively cultural exchange. It was in the midst of this exchange that Shatibi grew and learnt from a wide variety of religious scholars and linguists who were traveling through Granada, and specifically Jativa, because of its well-known paper production.

Shatibi's Cultural and Religious Education

In Granada, in Shatibi's time, there were two important religious institutions. First, there was the Great Mosque: People prayed there but it was also an academic institution where lectures were held. Secondly, there was the Nasserite School: Founded in the mid 1300s, this was an architecturally impressive school that also served as a place for scholars traveling through Granada to lecture. Many Andalusian and North African scholars taught and exchanged ideas at this institution (Abu al-Ajfan 1984: 29)

Therefore, even though political life was not stable in Granada, or indeed, in Muslim Spain in general at this time, Granada continued to be a lively metropolis that attracted scholars from different fields and from different parts of the Muslim world.

This rich cultural and intellectual milieu surrounded Shatibi in the 1300s.[1] Among the scholars who taught and influenced him were individuals from Andalusia, Loja, Granada and also many from Telmecen in North Africa. One of the major influences on Shatibi's thought and methodology was the philosopher Mohamed al-Farabi (Al-Raysouni 1991: 98).

This point brings us back to the introduction and the underlying argument in this paper; that there is no separation between the rational and irrational. Shatibi considered Farabi his second most important teacher. Even though Shatibi was a religious scholar and Farabi was preoccupied with philosophical issues, Shatibi still revered him as a scholar in his own right. Thus, the binary division between faith and rationality was not a concern to Shatibi. Shatibi did not see any contradiction between faith and reason.

Likewise, when Islamists call for a return to *sharia*, they see no contradiction between applying *sharia* and embracing modernity.

Shatibi's Works

Al-Muwafaqat

Shatibi's most famous contribution was in his book *Al-Muwafaqat* (The Agreements or The Agreed Upon). The naming of this book, according to Shatibi (*Al-Muwafaqat*: Part I: 24) was suggested by one of his contemporaries who felt that Muslim jurisconsults from different *Madhahib* (Muslim legal schools) would agree on what Shatibi had to say.

Al-Muwafaqat has won him fame right up until the present day because it is in this book that he writes about the sources of Islamic law and then links these to the theory/principle of *maqasid* (the end goals of *sharia*).[2]

Al-Itisam

This book was focused on the issue of heresy (*al-bida*) according to Islamic law. It draws extensively on legal principles such as *Maslaha* (public welfare) and *Istihsan*: A principle that is part of *Qiyas* (analogical reasoning).

Al-Ifadat wa al-Inshadat

This book is a literary book. Shatibi was a poet and therefore he published part of his poetry and literary works in it.

Kitab al-Majlis

This is Shatibi's only book on *fiqh* (Islamic jurisprudence). The book explains the application of Islamic law in property contracts. Shatibi also wrote *Al-Jalil* and *Sharh al-Alfiyah*. Both dealt with Arabic grammar and linguistics.

Before he wrote any of his books, Shatibi's fame and acknowledgment as a true scholar were dependent upon his methodology and his constant discussion and refutation with his contemporaries in Spain and North Africa. It is because Shatibi was so meticulous in gathering his legal information and discussing issues that he was not as prolific an author as his contemporaries (Raysouni 1981: 99).

Even though Shatibi sought consensus as a scholar, he was in direct opposition to some of the religious practices and norms of his society and some of his contemporary religious scholars. For example, Shatibi refused to conduct *du'a'* (pleading) after praying publicly in a group, or to mention and praise the four guided caliphs in his sermons, or to mention Imams in his sermons. Shatibi was also accused of being a conservative because he refused to take into consideration religious opinions (*fatwas*) that were weak, that is to say, those not widely known and accepted (Raysouni 1981: 102–3).

The Granadians and Andalusians who denounced Shatibi's practices were not his worst opponents: There were also religious scholars, like Abu Said Ibn Lobb, who accused Shatibi of heretic practices and cursed him publicly (Raysouni 1981: 103).

It is in this mood that Shatibi wrote his book *Al-Itisam*, which was one of his contributions in theory and practice on distinguishing and defining heresy.

THE RELEVANCE OF AL-MUWAFAQAT

So, after briefly introducing Shatibi's intellectual and cultural milieu, the discussion can now move on to focus on the contribution that he is still recognized for until the present day, namely his book, *Al-Muwafaqat* (The Agreements). The *Agreements'* importance stems basically from its emphasis on principles in Islamic law called "*maslaha*" (public welfare) and "*maqasid*" (the end goals of *sharia*).[3] His contribution in this text is mainly to legal theory (*Usul al-fiqh*).

The sources of Islamic law, or *usul al-fiqh* , are divided into two categories. One category is comprised of *al-nass* (the text), which consists of the Qur'an and the *sunna*. The other constitutes human judgement in several forms such as, for example, *Al-Ijma* (the consensus of the *fuqaha*) and *Al-Qiyas* (analogical reasoning).

Theoretically, therefore, there are two kinds of issues in *sharia*: *qatiyat* and *dhaniyat*. Issues that deal with *qatiyat* (definitive rules), are rules that are not changeable according to Islamic law, for example, times of prayer, fasting, alms giving and so on. The second type deals with *dhaniyat* (doubtful issues), that is to say, issues that allow for thought and speculation. Those issues are open to *Ijtihad* and those issues change with time and place—especially those issues pertaining to inter-human relationships.

A few scholars have recognized the importance of public welfare and the end goals of Islamic law, for example, Esposito writes:

> While all *fuqaha* came to accept the four sources of law, Islamic jurisprudence recognized other influences, designating them subsidiary principles of law. Among these were custom (*urf*), public interest (*istislah*), and jurist preference or equity (*istihsan*). In this way, some remnant of the inductive, human input that had characterized the actual methods of the law schools in their attempt to realize the *sharia's* primary concern with human welfare, justice and equity were acknowledged.
>
> (Esposito 1988: 34)

Sardar also stresses the importance of public welfare in Islamic law:

> Beyond these limited parameters, the *sharia* is completely open: it can be developed and shaped according to the needs of society and time by any number of its other sources: *al-ijma, al-qiyas, al-ijtihad* and *istislah*. The sources of the *sharia* that supplement the Qu'ran and the *sunna* are problem-solving tools; they provide a methodology for adjusting to change.
>
> (Sardar 1985: 114-5)

Aside from the few scholars who have recognized the importance of public welfare as a guiding Islamic legal principle, contemporary moderate Islamists have also stressed its importance. For example, Yusuf al-Qaradawi, a contemporary member of the Muslim Brotherhood and an activist addressed in this book, writes:

First, we need to investigate and analyze our cultural heritage in *fiqh* literature with its different schools and at different ages, in order to choose what will ensure the enforcement of *al-maqasid* (end goals of *sharia*) and the resurrection of *al-maslaha* (public welfare) in light of the changes taking place in contemporary life. Second, we need to go back to our roots: i.e. to the Qur'an and the *sunna*, to analyze it in light of *al-maqasid* (end goals of *sharia*). Third, we need to spend more effort in understanding contemporary issues that were not part of our ancestors' life, i.e. where the old *fuqaha* did not contribute to the issue as it relates to our modern times.

(Qaradawi 1973: 108–9)

Qaradawi also writes:

If one takes a verse from the Qur'an or any particular *hadith*, without relating it to *al-maqasid* (the end goals of *sharia*), one is likely to misunderstand and misinterpret the *sharia*. This is why al-Imam al-Shatibi in his book *al-Muwafaqat*, insisted that to understand *al-sharia* one has to comprehend and know its end goals. This only happens when one is knowledgeable about the verses of the Qur'an and the Hadith; why, how and when they were revealed, the reason behind revelation, which *hadiths* are eternal and which were temporal ... etc.

(Qaradawi 1981: 152)

Ghanouchi, another activist discussed in this book and the leader of the Renaissance Party (*al-Nahda*), indicates that "the end goals of *sharia* should provide a legal basis for future Muslim societies" (Darwish 1992: 130–9).

Turabi agrees:

Worship is the most inclusive of all end goals of *sharia*. The end goals of *sharia* are in agreement with another source of jurisprudential reasoning and that is *istishab* (using precedence from other cases until opposite rules prove to be better for the common good). *Istishab* promotes gradual change, i.e. it does not negate all that came before Islam and generate a totally new system, and *istishab* is a state of continuous change. Therefore if we combine *istishab* with *al-masalih* (public welfare) we will find the essence of public life in Islam.

(Turabi 1980: 26)

Even Islamic extremists like Sheikh Umar Abdel Rahman has written:

The role of the learned people is a very important one, in the Islamic world. It is their role to guide the Islamic movement: to adapt to modernity and the realities of life and at the same time to concur with Islamic law and its end goals (*al-maqasid*).

(Umar Abdel Rahman 1989: 154)

The principle of public welfare stresses the importance of developing Islamic law based on the idea that good is lawful and that lawful must be good. It basically enables Islamic law to adapt and change according to the time and place it exists in. Public welfare also integrates the use of human reasoning in the application of Islamic law (without crossing the realm of *Qatiyat* (Absolutes) that are clearly stated in the Textual sources).

Thus, the principle connotes issues such as modernity, civil society, and governance according to Islamic law and Islamic mores. By implication, public welfare and preserving the mind, religion, self, posterity and wealth are the essence of the ideal Islamic state.

CONCLUSION

Shatibi's influence on the remnants of Muslim Spain are well recognized in the legacy that he left to his students, individuals like Abu Yehya Ibn Asim, Abu Bakr al-Kady, and Abu Abdallah al-Bayani (Abu Al-Ajfan 1984: 40). His observance and stress on public welfare also led the people to question elements of habitualized practices that were detached in spirit from their faith. His scrutiny of certain public practices was met with resistance, however, his theoretical contribution to the sources of Islamic law (*Usul al-Fiqh*) activated religious inquiry in Muslim Spain and it still continues to engage contemporaries.

Furthermore, Shatibi was a unique scholar in his day and age, given his *fatwas* (legal opinion). For example, people went to Shatibi asking him about his legal opinion of a Bedouin woman who was teaching the Qur'an to other women and girls. Shatibi responded that if she knew how to read it without making any mistakes and if she did not sing the Qur'an instead of just reciting it, then her teaching was valuable. Shatibi added, however, that what was common to a lot of women, as well as men, was that they did not read the Qur'an accurately (Abou al-Ajfan 1984: 122). Shatibi appreciated the Bedouin women's efforts (provided that she stuck to the rules of recitation) and he also equated men and women in their poor knowledge of reading the Qur'an accurately. That is to say, he did not discriminate against the Bedouin on the basis of her gender.

In another fatwa, Shatibi responded to a North African scholar who discussed the problem of being distracted during prayers. The North African scholar said that if a person was thinking about something during prayers, the person should get rid of whatever preoccupied him, even if it was worth 50 thousand dirhams. Shatibi responded that if everyone followed this fatwa, everyone would lose everything they owned and their families! Then, what if the person was preoccupied with his poverty and his plight? How would he get rid of that during prayers? (Raysouni 1991: 119–20).

Obviously, Shatibi was not of the opinion that Muslims should not pay attention to prayers. However, he was utilizing a very important principle in the legal interpretation of Islamic laws and mores:

> If following the rules and mores, generally, leads the person to hardship (hardship that the law and human reason do not accept), then the rule of the law could not be generalized in its applicability.
> (Shatibi, *Al-Muwafaqat*: Part I: 102)

In line with the rest of his writings, Shatibi stresses here that there are exceptions to the rule. For example, if the rule leads to extreme hardship, that hardship goes against the essence and spirit of the law.

In conclusion, I would like to restate that the binary division between faith and reason was not part of the Muslim understanding and ethos. On the contrary, what Shatibi seems to argue in his contributions to the sources of Islamic law (*Usul al-Fiqh*) is that faith and reason are complementary to each other.

As a scholar, Shatibi's contributions in the fourteenth century were relevant in his lifetime, after his death, and up until today.

In an article published in Boston Review, Khaled Abou el-Fadl writes about the compatibility of Islam and Democracy, using notions reminiscent of Shatibi's works. In response to Abou el-Fadl's article, John Esposito writes:

> Modern reformers in the twentieth century began to reinterpret key traditional Islamic concepts and institutions: consultation (*shura*) of rulers with those ruled, consensus (*ijma*) of the community, rein-

terpretation (*ijtihad*), and legal principles such as the public welfare
(*maslaha*) of society to develop Islamic forms of parliamentary
governance, representative elections, and religious reform. Reformers
in the twenty-first century, like Khaled Abou el-Fadl, continue the
process in diverse ways.

(Esposito 2003: bostonreview.net)

Shatibi's legacy and contribution to Muslim Spain did not
end with his death. His ideas and principles still provide
researchers and reformists with a wealth of tools to analyze,
examine and finally apply Islamic law in our day and age.
Amongst the people who utilize Shatibi and other similar
jurisprudential writings are contemporary moderate Islamists
like Qaradawi, Ghannouchi and Yassine—who are the
forthcoming focus of my research and analyses.

3
Yusuf al-Qaradawi:
Modernization is Key

The Islamic Movement will not have a rational political ideology unless it overcomes these negative ideological phenomena and their effects on people. It must also nurture this new type of fiqh[1] that we are focusing on—the fiqh of the end goals of Sharia[2], the fiqh of balance and the fiqh of priorities.

(Qaradawi 2000: 154)

This chapter focuses on the thought of Yusuf al-Qaradawi and the experiences that shaped it. He is a major exponent of a centrist position and of a democracy based on tenets of Islamic faith and informed by Islamic history. The three sections of Chapter 3 include his life story, the development of his theoretical approach to knowledge and democracy, and the conclusion—that his positions support a robust, non-Western style democratic state.

QARADAWI'S LIFE AND UPBRINGING

Youth

As related in his autobiography (Qaradawi 2002), Qaradawi grew up in Saft al-Turab. The mosque was the most important institution in his village, and religious scholars were most influential. However, reverence toward these scholars did not inhibit people from freely voicing their opinions. Qaradawi describes an incident during which one of the Azhar-educated scholars blamed the villagers for their ignorance. In response, the outraged villagers cursed him while he was giving his sermon.

Qaradawi comes from a modest background. His father, Abd-Allah, who died when Qaradawi was two years old, worked both in trade and as a peasant. After his father's death, Qaradawi's uncle took care of him. His mother's side of the family were merchants and they were relatively better off than his father's relatives. He grew up in the homes of his father's family and his maternal grandfather.

Qaradawi received his first schooling in *al-Kutab*, a linguistic/religious elementary education that is common in villages of many Muslim countries.[3] He was able to learn all of the Qur'an by heart at the tender age of nine, making him the youngest student to have done so in his village. At seven, he began his secular education in state schools, finishing at the age of twelve. To prepare for matriculation at al-Azhar University, he then attended high school at a religious institute.

At this point Qaradawi began giving sermons and leading people in prayers, embarking upon a religious career as a scholar in his own village. After high school, he went on to the religious institute in Tanta where he experienced some independence, living with two other youths from his family.

During his first year in Tanta, Qaradawi's political life began. He describes "two incidents in my first year in Tanta that later shaped my future: 1) listening to a lecture by Al-Sheikh Hasan al-Banna[4], 2) the death of my mother." Despite this blow, Qaradawi ended the year at the top of his class. In his second year, he got to know Bahi al-Khuli,

a product of Dar al-'Ulum and a classmate and friend of
Banna's. At the end of this year, he delivered his first religious
sermon, one of the landmarks in his life.

In his fourth year of college, Qaradawi was invited by the
Muslim Brothers to open a conference with some of his poetry.
Following his recitation, a Muslim Brother approached him
to become a member. He gladly accepted the offer and filled
out a membership application.

After four years at al-Azhar, Qaradawi continued on to
secondary school, called *al-Thanawiya* in Arabic. Among
his many new teachers was the well known Egyptian scholar
Al-Sheikh al-Sha'rawi.[5] From the exchanges between Sha'rawi
and Qaradawi we learn much about Shar'awi's thoughts
opposing the Muslim Brotherhood. He appears to have been
very sensitive about challenges to his authority on this issue.
When Qaradawi asked Sha'rawi a question he responded:
"Listen Yousef, if you think you are as powerful as the wind,
you have just met the tornado."

Years later, in 1997, Sha'rawi revealed to Qaradawi that
he had been warned against the Muslim Brotherhood and
the students who followed them.

In his biography, Qaradawi discusses how he was taught
"modern science" at al-Azhar, a topic central to the analysis
in this study of the relationship, or choice, between faith
and reason. He argues that "modern science" is a misnomer,
because many scientific principles were explained by Muslim
scholars in the dawn of Islam. In discussing the relationship
of the sciences to Islamic faith, Qaradawi emphasizes that:

> In many instances, religious scholars were also scholars of the sciences
> and nature. They never felt hindered by their faith; on the contrary
> their faith encouraged them to excel in those sciences.

> I remember Fakhr al-Razi who excelled in both religion and
> medicine. Also, Ibn al-Nafis who discovered the circulatory system
> and was as effective as a *faqih* (religious scholar). Likewise, Ibn Rushd,
> who exceeded in Philosophy, Medicine, Law and religious studies.
>
> (Qaradawi 2002: 233)

In Qaradawi's view, there is no conflict between faith and
reason or religion and the sciences.

Participation and Membership of the Muslim Brotherhood

Qaradawi continued to attend meetings with Banna and
the Muslim Brothers in Tanta. He observed how Banna's
nationalist call for justice unified Egyptians whether they were
Muslims or Copts. For example, Naseef Khalil, a Copt, who
was knowledgeable about Egyptian rights to the Suez Canal,
always joined Banna in his lectures. Banna was unfailingly
cordial to Coptic leaders who were made part of the Political
Committee of the Muslim Brotherhood and were included
in decision making.

Qaradawi's closest personal encounter with Banna occurred
when Qaradawi wrote some poetry praising him (which was
collected by Banna's secretary). Qaradawi followed Banna
through many governorates as he delivered his speeches. He
also continued his active *da'wa* as well as writing poetry,
especially on occasions such as the twentieth anniversary of
the founding of the Muslim Brotherhood (1948). He wrote:

> Oh *da'wa* of truth tell people what you have found, for at times the
> truth suffers while deception is hailed.
>
> You have been born when the East is depressed because of lost
> rights, even though the West is joyful and arrogant.
>
> The rights of the shameless are accepted and respected, while the
> rights of the religious go unnoticed.

They thought that the bearded are insane, but wait—behind the beards are the strong and the feisty.

To the West they are the end, to the East they are the hope for abetting the faith and freeing the nation.

(Qaradawi 2002: 305)

Qaradawi writes about the Muslim Brotherhood and how it influenced him:

1. It helped me understand Islam better, for it is religious and worldly, faith and law, worship and leadership, the Qur'an and the sword.

2. I became aware of the importance of collective action in reviewing the faith and its position in society.

3. I shifted from being personally religious, to proselytizing the faith in nearby villages, to finally being a Muslim *da'iya* (missionary).

4. I shifted from personal worries to worries about the nation and the Islamic *Umma*. My ambitions went beyond personal gains to more fulfilling ambitions of freeing Egypt, the Arabs, and the Muslims from foreign occupation (mentally, legally, and physically).

5. One of the dangers that plagued Egypt at the time was the divide between intellectuals who were taught at al-Azhar (religiously inclined) and intellectuals who were taught at King Farouq's University (secularly inclined). However, the Muslim Brotherhood was able to bridge that divide so that there were no more complications between the people who wore Islamic head gear (sheikhs) and the people of the fezzes (effendis).

(Qaradawi 2002: 314–7)

In late 1948, Banna allegedly lost control of the secret apparatus of the Muslim Brotherhood. The year 1949 was to bring the demise of the Muslim Brotherhood's society and the death of its populist leader Hassan al-Banna.

Impact of the Dissolution of the Muslim Brotherhood

On December 8, 1948, the king ordered the dissolution of the Muslim Brotherhood. Qaradawi cites Banna's account:

A report was handed to Nuqrashi Pasha from the British and French
embassies, as well as the US diplomatic representative, recommending
the dissolution of the Muslim Brotherhood. This recommendation was
a result of a meeting in Fayed on December 6, 1948.

(Qaradawi 2002: 324)

In response to this decree, violence broke out for which the
incumbent government held the Muslim Brothers responsible.[6]
Indiscriminate round ups and imprisonment of thousands of
Muslim Brothers ensued, including torture in prisons and
violation of all human rights. On February 12, 1949, Banna
was assassinated.[7]

During the turmoil, Qaradawi and his friends hid in one of
their houses. However, when the mother of one was arrested
and imprisoned, they all went to the police station to turn
themselves in. Qaradawi was imprisoned in Tanta for 40
days, and then transferred first to a Cairo prison called the
Heixtap, and then to Suez where a ship called Aida awaited
him and the rest of the Muslim Brothers. The ship would
take them to Tor (used as a quarantine city, before travelers
were allowed to enter the cities and governorates of Egypt).

The imprisoned Muslim Brothers quickly organized
themselves, choosing Al-Sheikh al-Ghazali as their leader.
His first action was to organize a demonstration protesting
about malnutrition in the prison. It persuaded the head of the
prison to agree to give the Muslim Brothers appropriate raw
materials to cook for themselves. The prison quickly turned
into a Muslim Brotherhood camp ground where discipline
and order reigned. Each member fulfilled a shifting roster of
daily responsibilities such as cooking or cleaning.

Qaradawi and the rest of the Muslim Brothers enjoyed
organizing themselves and their days in prison. They regularly
awoke one hour before al-*Fajr* (dawn) prayers, after which the

brothers would break into lecture groups, and the *mashayekh*[8] would deliver their lectures. By sunrise, the brothers would be ready for their hour of physical exercise followed by breakfast. After breakfast, each unit/group would finish its chores. They met for *al-dohr* (noon) prayers, then lunch, then siesta. Later, they would pray *al-'Asr* (late afternoon) prayers. After those prayers, the brothers would return to their lectures and group discussions which continued until al-Maghreb (sunset) prayers. The brothers would have a light meal before praying *al-'Isha* (evening) prayers and finally go to sleep for the night.[9]

Though orderly, the situation was far from ideal. For example, among the brothers were the "*basabis*", a nickname given by the brothers to spies planted among them by the government to report their activities. The spies were quickly discovered by the brothers since they did not particularly appreciate waking up for the sunrise prayers and they were not conscientious about the rest of the prayers either.

To their disappointment, Qaradawi and his classmates at al-Azhar were soon moved from Tor back to the Heixtap prison in Cairo. Their long and difficult journey from Tor to Heixtap also left an indelible mark in their lives. Life in the Cairo prison was more difficult than at Tor. They managed to start studying for their final examinations, although prison officials would not allow the students to sit them.

Following the 1952 revolution, Qaradawi and the other Muslim Brothers were released from prison. He quickly returned to his studies and took his exams within two weeks, earning second place on the national level.

University Student Years in Cairo

Qaradawi moved to Cairo to continue his studies at al-Azhar University. In addition to religious topics, he studied history,

Greek philosophy, Asian philosophy, Islamic philosophy, psychology, logic, and the English language.

At this juncture he broadened his focus, previously confined to religious issues, to include a different and wider range of interests stimulated by the cultural and intellectual life of Cairo. During this period, he met with the visiting Sheikh Abu al-Hassan al-Nadawi of India and introduced him to some of the Muslim Brothers.

Life in Cairo was expensive, especially for a student like Qaradawi. Seeking employment in al-Mahala, he found work in a new mosque that was still under construction. The Muslim Brothers provided Qaradawi with a simple room in al-Mahala and in Cairo. His popularity and the *khutab* (speeches) that he gave quickly enhanced the reputation of the mosque. Soon, the number of people praying outside the mosque was double the number of those praying inside the building. People from Tanta, Samanoud, Talkha, and Mansoura gathered to hear Qaradawi's sermons.

Life After Imprisonment

While studying and preaching, Qaradawi earned a Masters degree in Qur'an and *Sunna* Studies in 1960 and a Ph.D. in 1973.[10] He taught in several mosques and directed the Imam Institute. He also worked in the Islamic Cultural Department at al-Azhar University. As early as 1961 he became the dean of Qatar's School of Religion. After obtaining his doctorate, he continued his work in Qatar in the newly-created college, which later became Qatar University.

Qaradawi was the founder and chair of the Islamic Studies Department at Qatar. He developed and headed the Islamic Legal Studies Program in 1977 and also created a "Sunna and Sira" Research Center which he continues to direct. In recognition of these efforts, he has received many accolades: An award from the Islamic Development Bank for his work on Islamic Economics and King Faisal's award for his contribution to this topic in Islamic Studies. Qaradawi continues to teach and appear on al-Jazeera Network on a weekly show called *al-Sharia wa al-Hayat* (Life and Islamic Law). He also contributes on a regular basis to his personal website.

QARADAWI'S THEORETICAL APPROACH
TO KNOWLEDGE AND DEMOCRACY

The Renaissance and Enlightenment eras in Europe separated scientific theory and practice from faith. The history of Western civilization includes many examples of power struggles provoked by new scientific theories, particularly in the seventeenth and eighteenth centuries. As the authority of the Catholic Church and its cumulative episteme were challenged by the rise of new discoveries, it is not surprising that the church persecuted and excommunicated those who challenged official dogma.

As discussed earlier, this affected the role the church played in the Western world in the post-Enlightenment era. Not only was the church increasingly removed from public life, but also the foundations of the faith itself were subjected to questioning. The conflict between faith and science also dictated the way societies organized themselves politically and economically. The popular perception of democracy is that it is founded on the need to separate Church and State.

In this intellectual context, it is essential to examine what and how Qaradawi thinks about scientific advancement and the questioning and examination of the faith. His perception of the role of science is key to understanding his view of the place and role of religion in public life.

Reason, Science and Faith: Their Roles and their Respective Expanse

In a translation of Qaradawi's *Priorities of the Islamic Movement in the Coming Phase* (2000), he states:

> Belief to us Muslims is not against reason or intellect. On the contrary, it is based on and fed by the intellect, and the believers are described in the Qur'an as 'men of understanding', and the Qur'an itself is a sign for 'people who understand' or 'people who ponder'. *Aql* (intellect and reason), to the prominent intellectuals of the *Umma* is the basis of *naql* (inherited revealed knowledge); for without it nobody could have proved the existence of Allah or the validity of Prophethood. Through the instructions it contains, the Qur'an has laid down the foundation of the 'scientific mentality' which worships Allah with the *aql* and believes with evidence and denounces the imitation of forefathers or prominent figures.
>
> (Qaradawi 2000: 112)

In describing the needs of future generations in the Islamic movement, he clarifies that "scientific ideology" does not necessarily mean or refer to the applied sciences alone. He explains that it is: "an ideology that would not accept any claim without proof, any result without a preamble and would not accept evidence which is not definitive and free from suspicion" (Qaradawi 2000: 113). Qaradawi describes the attributes of the "scientific spirit" as:

> 1) Being objective in seeking knowledge and truth, regardless of its source.

2) Acknowledging different fields of specialization. For example, religious scholars are to be respected for their knowledge of the faith. However, political and economics specialists should be given space to examine and conduct their research and to make recommendations for their societies.

3) Maintaining the ability to criticize oneself and learn from past mistakes.

4) Utilizing the latest techniques and knowledge in any given area of specialization regardless of its source.

5) Examining and contesting everything with the exception of 'religious and intellectual incontestable facts'.

6) Examining meticulously and cross-examining issues as necessary before adopting or disregarding the issue at hand.

7) Tolerating opposing viewpoints concerning opinions and ideas that pertain to 'ijtihad'[11].

(Qaradawi 2000: 113–5)

In critique of modern Orientalists, Qaradawi writes:

Their usual points of departure made them examine what was not subject to testing, from their point of view, as they believe that the Qur'an was not sent down by Allah and that Muhammed is not the Messenger of Allah. In this way, they form their ideas in advance, prior to starting their research. They then take their research in such a direction that may enable them to prove these ideas by any means, thereby accepting narratives of poor credibility, believing lies, magnifying small events and making a mountain out of a molehill. They even take suspicion as evidence and reject all that contradicts their ideas even if it hits them in the face!

(Qaradawi 2000: 215)

Turning the table on those who criticize Islam and Islamists for rigidity and intolerance, he points out that Orientalists also impose judgment without any scientific proofs for their assertions and arguments.

Qaradawi contends that "*al-dhan*" (doubt) is detested in the Qur'an and that passions and subjectivity are contrary to the scientific spirit that is needed for the future of Muslim societies. Scientific claims require *burhan* (proof). He utilizes the Qur'an to further argue his abhorrence of "*al-dhan*": "Tell them to come forth with their proofs if they are truthful" (Surat al-Baqara: Aya 111).

"It is not acceptable," he states, "that in the twenty first century, the Islamists do not utilize statistics to prove their claims." He criticizes Islamists who rely on emotional speeches to convince people of their ideas: "Our age dictates the use of statistics and scientific methods—this is what differentiates the learned from the sophists and the brazen" (Qaradawi 2002: 109–10).

Even though Qaradawi is critical of the Orientalists, he recognizes the works of Gustave Lebonne who said that: "Arabs were the first people to exercise the unison between free thinking and religious piety" (Qaradawi 2001a: 173).

In 1996, Qaradawi said—emphasizing the strong link between reason and faith: "For us, science is religion and religion is science" (Baker 2003: 48).

According to Baker, Yusuf al-Qaradawi took the lead in explaining precisely why the linguistic character of the message of the Qur'an required reasoned interpretation and not mechanical application. "God wanted some of his provisions to be clearly stated and others left unspoken," wrote Qaradawi. Clearly, implicit meanings could only be deduced by the mind (Baker 2003: 105).

Qaradawi practises his preaching by adopting numerous technological venues to express his opinions. He provided the major intellectual force for the influential Islam Online Internet site, and he was also one of the first Islamic intellectuals to establish his own website, which attracted an impressive global response. At the same time, Qaradawi's regular program on al Jazeera channel secured him a prominent place in the new Arab satellite media (Baker 2003: 267).

Ijtihad and Tajdid

Qaradawi furthers his argument regarding faith and reason by addressing the eminently important questions of *ijtihad* and *tajdid*. *Ijtihad* is making the effort and, in this context, it means to reinterpret Islamic law where there is an allowance for reinterpretation. *Tajdid* is literally "renewal" and, in this context, it also refers to the reinterpretation and renewal of Islamic law.

The stress on *ijtihad* and *tajdid* in Qaradawi's writing is unparalleled in the work of other Islamists. All of his books discuss these concepts. This perspective reveals a natural progression from stating that reason and faith are non-conflictual to seeking a definition of their relationship and encouraging the renewal of human efforts in appreciating the faith.

Qaradawi's interests in *tajdid* are numerous, including concern for the blind adoption of cultural values from the "secular West" or from the "atheist East" (Qaradawi 2001a: 32). He draws attention to the dangers of the academic milieu in the Middle East, in which he sees liberal and Marxist values praised as the only examples to be followed.

Qaradawi recommends the cultivation of a new breed of *mujtahids*. They should be able to:

1) master the Arabic language,
2) have a strong theological background,
3) be capable of differentiating between absolute teachings and the issues that could be subjected to human interpretation,

4) be close to the people, that is to say, they cannot 'live in their
ivory towers and disconnect with the peoples needs and the times
they live in'.

(Qaradawi 2001a: 46)

He envisions that this process of renaissance and renewal
could characterize more than a few *mujtahids*. He sees
their numbers growing into an assembly or congregation of
international *Fiqh* specialists who practice *ijtihad* freely, away
from political and mob pressures (Qaradawi 2001a: 50).

In his effort to clarify the role of *ijtihad* in Muslim societies,
he writes that his worst fear for the Islamic Movement is that
it opposes the free thinkers among its followers and closes the
door to *tajdid* and *ijtihad*, confining itself to only one type of
thinking that does not accept any other viewpoints, objectives,
or means. Qaradawi emphasizes that human *ijtihad* is always
subject to development and change according to the changing
conditions and factors (Qaradawi 2000: 133).

The renewal that is called for by Qaradawi focuses on
familiarity and knowledge of *fiqh al-sunan*[12] and the *fiqh*
of the end goals of Islamic law: As far as Qaradawi is
concerned the Islamic Movement will not have a rational
political ideology unless it overcomes the negative ideological
phenomena that influence the process of religious deduction.
Qaradawi thinks that Islamic activists should nurture the *fiqh*
of the *sunan*, the *fiqh* of the end-goals of the *sharia*, the *fiqh*
of balance and the *fiqh* of priorities (Qaradawi 2000: 154).

Baker also notes Qaradawi's regard for *ijtihad*. He notes
that, in a key passage in *The Islamic Awakening*, Qaradawi
sums up the heart of the "new Islamist" case against the
textualists. He explains that "had He so desired, God could
have given all religion the same formulation, unquestionable

and needing no *ijtihad*, so that those who disobey would immediately make themselves unbelievers".

Qaradawi begins his broad argument for the necessity of reasoned *ijtihad* with the essentials of the faith that not even the most extreme elements question. The source of Islam, he notes, is the Qur'an and the *sunna*. The Qur'an is a group of texts, and most of the *sunna* consists of texts as well. Observing the distinctive position of the "new Islamists", Qaradawi comments that "these texts of [the] Qur'an and [the] *sunna* are just like any other language text as far as understanding and interpretation are concerned". The texts use "the words and structure of the language". For Qaradawi and the "new Islamists", the implications are clear: "Some words," he writes, "can have more than one meaning. Others can be understood literally, figuratively, or metaphorically."

"The unspoken always yields disagreements," writes Qaradawi. From a vantage point that rejects the kinds of misplaced certitude and absolutism shown by the extremists, he adds with unmistakable emphasis, "difference is a treasure because it triggers different *ijtihad* by different *ulama*, and with this, *fiqh* is immeasurably enriched" (Baker 2003: 105–6).

Qaradawi clearly states that Muslims have the right to interpret their faith in a wide array of matters that pertain to social, political and economic practices. Their only restriction is to abide by the end goals of Islamic law, these intended to uphold public welfare and guard individuals as well (Qaradawi 2001b: 64–5).

He was also extremely critical of extremist interpretations of the faith. He points out that there are two theological groups in Islam that support *tajmeed*[13]. Firstly, there are the imitators of old interpreters from different Islamic schools

of law (*Madhahib*). These groups uphold their interpretations and refuse to accept other interpretations whether such
interpretation has been done by a group or an individual.
The second group is the new *Dhahiriya*[14] and those who are
superficial in their interpretations of the faith. Their interpretations of the faith stop at the letter of the law and do not
encompass the spirit or the end goals of the law.

Both groups fight fiercely over negligible issues in Islam.
"They are like a mother who kills her child by locking him/
her up because she's afraid the sun and the wind might hurt
them" (Qaradawi 2001a: 51).

Al-Wasat: On Being a Centrist

One of the most important positions that Qaradawi
proclaims as his own in modern Islamic discourse is the
"centrist disposition".[15] This is the moderate/median stance
between secularists and Islamic extremists. This position
takes advantage of the rich Islamic principles of *muwazana*[16]
and *maslaha*.[17]

Qaradawi writes of his "centrist" position in his book
Al-Sahwa al-Islamiya (The Islamic Awakening) (Qaradawi
1998: 35–84). He explains his:

1) centrist position between old versus new interpretations of the
faith,
2) centrist stance between what is static versus dynamic in the faith,
and
3) centrist discourse between extreme versus lax interpretations of
Islam.

He writes that a rational political ideology is only possible
if Muslim societies advocate the use of *fiqh'ul-muwazanat*
and *fiqh'ul maslaha* amongst others (Qaradawi 2000: 154).

Qaradawi's centrist position has translated into a political party in Egypt, the Wasat Party, wherein the young Islamists "... have absorbed both Qaradawi's view that Islam is broader than religion and Abul Magd's arguments that civilizational Islam provides the generous foundations for a pluralistic and inclusive national project". They explain that their "use of the term civilizational Islam does not reject Islam as a religion; on the contrary, religion is part of it and adds to it" (Baker 2003: 193).

Qaradawi's centrist position is also clear in his discussions of the Taliban. As rulers in the name of Islam, the Taliban had responsibilities to the world of Islam. Qaradawi did not hesitate to say that they were failing to meet them in egregious ways. A regime is Islamic by the measure of its progress toward justice, Islam's core value. In failing so completely to meet that standard, the Taliban had "broken our hearts", Qaradawi said, "with their backward and violent ways that caused terrible damage to the name of Islam everywhere" (Baker 2003: 239).

Qaradawi's efforts to distinguish himself as a centrist are not just theoretical. He extends his religious and legal opinions to his practice as a religious leader. His fatwa (legal opinion) concerning the Buddha statues of Afghanistan is another case in point that translates his theoretical centrist position into action: He advised the Taliban not to tear down the statues because they are part of the country's cultural heritage. He used the legal precedence of 'Amr Ibn al-'Aas when he conquered Egypt. He did not tear down the Pyramids, the Sphinx, or any Pharaonic relics (Baker 2003: 78–9).

Qaradawi's opinion regarding the utilization of reason, his call for a renewal of the faith and engaging in *ijtihad*, along with his moderate approach to understanding and practising the law all lead us to the impassioned question of democracy.[18]

Qaradawi's Views on Democracy

As early as 1993, Qaradawi issued a few religious opinions (*fatwas*) concerning democracy. He spoke for all the "new Islamists" when he unambiguously embraced political pluralism, including the competition of political parties. He explicitly rejected the contrary views of Hassan al Banna, founder of the Muslim Brothers. Reasoning by analogy, Qaradawi explained that Islam has no trouble tolerating diversity in *sharia*, recognizing four major schools as authoritative, despite important differences among them. Clearly, Islam could and should, value pluralism in the political sphere. With the same emphasis, Qaradawi took as a starting point the Islamic notion of *shura*[19] through which the ruler provides a secure conceptual anchor for contemporary efforts to build democracy. Again, with the full support of the "new Islamists", Qaradawi unequivocally pronounced that *shura* was obligatory and not voluntary (Baker 2003: 173).

Even though Qaradawi's opinions in speech and writing are favorable to democracy he, like many Islamists, is wary of the "Western" version. He writes:

> ... some Islamists still have their reservations on democracy and are even wary of the word 'democracy' itself. What I wish to stress here is that Islam is not democracy and democracy is not Islam. I would rather that Islam is not wedded to any political principle or system. Islam is unique in its means, ends, and methodologies. I do not wish Western democracy to be imposed on us with its bad ideologies and values unless we add to it our own values and ideologies, so that we can integrate it into our comprehensive system.
>
> (Qaradawi 2000: 187–8)

However in the same work Qaradawi states:

> A closer look at the history of the Muslim *umma* and the Islamic Movement in modern times should show clearly that the Islamic Ideology, the Islamic Movement and the Islamic Awakening have never flourished or borne fruit unless in an atmosphere of democracy and freedom, and have withered and become barren only at times of oppression and tyranny that trod over the will of the people who clung to Islam. Such oppressive regimes imposed their Secularism, Socialism, or Communism on their people by force and coercion, using covert torture and public executions, and employing those devilish tools that tore flesh, shed blood, crushed bones and destroyed souls.
>
> Therefore, I would not imagine that the Islamic Movement could support anything other than political freedom and democracy.
>
> However, the tools and guaranties created by democracy are as close as can ever be to the realization of the political principles brought to this world by Islam to put a leash on the ambitions and whims of rulers. These principles are: *shura*, *nasihah* (advice), enjoining the good and forbidding the evil, disobeying illegal orders, resisting unbelief, and changing wrong by force when possible. It is only in democracy and political freedom that the power of parliament is evident and that people's deputies can withdraw confidence from any government that breaches the constitution. It is, also, only in such an environment that the strength of free press, free parliament, opposition and the masses are most felt.
>
> (Qaradawi 2000: 187–8)

At first glance Qaradawi's opinions might seem contradictory. However, his full fledged support for democracy does not run counter to his conscientious doubts about the "Western" form. Like many Muslims, he differentiates between the historical experience of the West, that is the separation between church and state as the cornerstone of modernity and state building, versus the Muslim experience that does not share this historical narrative. For Qaradawi, the adoption of democratic mores is acceptable, as long as they are separated from the way they were originally generated. In this view, the goal of democracy is a virtue, but many roads may lead to it. The Western historical experience and the separation of church and state do not have to be replicated.

Qaradawi clarifies that he is not calling for a theocracy:

> It is a mistake to think that the Islamic State I am calling for is a religious state. It is a civil state that is built on choices, elections, political participation and the accountability of the ruler to the ruled. This state provides each of its members with the right to advise the ruler, to enjoin him from harm and to command him towards public welfare. A ruler in Islam is bound by God's laws. A ruler is not the deputy of God, he is the deputy of the Muslim state, i.e. he is chosen by the members of the state, and the members watch over him, hold him accountable, and impeach him if they so deem.
>
> (Qaradawi 2001b: 58–9)

Hakimiyat–Allah is sometimes incorrectly translated as "God's Rule". According to Islamic literalists and the Western interpretation, it is an Islamic State that is run as a theocracy such as, for example, post 1979 Iran. However, the literalist/ extremist view of a future Islamic state is less popular in many parts of the Muslim world.

In response to the literalists, Qaradawi explains that the term "God's Rule" refers to ruling according to God's laws, that is Sharia. However, political authority is an issue that is decided by the people: "The people choose their rulers, they hold them accountable, they observe them, and they impeach them if need be" (Qaradawi 2001b: 62).

Qaradawi negates and strives to prove that neither Qutb nor Mawdudi meant *Hakimiya* as modern extremists have interpreted it. He writes that it is very important to distinguish between a ruler's authority and the authority of God manifested in Islamic law. That is to say, a ruler could not change religious rites, such as times of prayers and style of prayer—which fall under a very limited and focused area of Islamic law called the "Absolutes" (*Al-Qat'iyat*). However, the ruler and the people have the right to interpret and decide questions concerning everyday life, such as social, economic, and political policies—so long as they do not go against the spirit of Islamic law in general. The vast area that is open to interpretation, called the "unmentioned" or the "doubtfuls" (*Al-Maskut 'Anhu* or *al-Dhaniyat*), is where human interpretation steps in to respond to cultural differences and the change in time and place of applying Islamic law (Qaradawi 2001b: 64–5, Abdelkader 2000 and 2003).

Qaradawi moves beyond legitimating democracy as an ideal to examining it from an Islamic legal perspective:

> There is nothing in Islamic law that prohibits adopting ideas and systems from others as long as those ideas are not in conflict with the basic tenets of the faith. Therefore we could adopt democracy; we could adopt its ways and mechanisms; however, we have the right to amend it and change it to suit our needs and our culture.
>
> (Qaradawi 2001b: 138)

Democracy means that the people rule themselves. There is no conflict between people ruling themselves (which is the cornerstone of democracy) and *Hakimiyat-Allah* (which is the basis of Islamic canon).

In the discourse on democracy, people choose their rulers, they hold them accountable, and they refuse to follow the ruler when he goes against Islamic law. In Islamic terms, if the ruler goes against Islamic law, continues to disregard the people's advice, or sways from justice and fair conduct, the people should impeach him (Qaradawi 2001b: 139).

In a more recent publication, Qaradawi re-emphasizes the importance of appropriating democracy:

> Muslims should agree on means of peaceful change, they should make use of the democratic mechanisms of change. The faithful should always seek wisdom regardless of its origin. There is no shame in adopting other people's ways if they are beneficial to the Muslim in this world and in the hereafter, as long as those mechanisms are not in contradiction to Islamic law. On the contrary, those mechanisms are part and parcel of the public welfare and the end goals of Islamic law (al-Maqasid).
>
> (Qaradawi 2002: 326)

CONCLUSION

Qaradawi's insistence on a centrist position in understanding and interpreting Islam is a key factor in comprehending the contemporary populist stance of Islamic activism. He champions the reinterpretation of the faith pertaining to contemplative issues like rulership and governance.

Qaradawi's openness to adopting the mechanisms of democracy is also essential to understanding contemporary Islamic activism. Within the context of Qaradawi's life experience, his perception of the role of faith in public life is central to grievances against incumbent Muslim regimes.

In essence, his discourse about faith and reason provides a solid understanding of the degree to which each should be applied in public life. First and foremost, he finds no conflict between reason and faith. Second, while reason should always be used, it should never go against the Nass (textual sources), if there are any. Examination of the sources, that is to say, the texts, and taking a moderate position against extremes (*al-ghuluw*) lies at the heart of Qaradawi's argument.

This liberal outlook and encouragement of *ijtihad* (reinterpretation of textual sources) strongly support his advocacy of a moderate Islamic state. Qaradawi is a good example of an "anti-American democrat": An Islamic thinker who prefers to create a new amalgam of western political processes in the service of Islamic principles and culture.[20]

Does Qaradawi's advocacy of *ijtihad*, *al-wasatiya*, and *al-Maqasid*, equate to our perception of Western liberal democracy?

4
Rachid al-Ghannouchi: Minorities and Equality

This chapter concentrates on the life and thought of Rachid al-Ghannouchi. He is the founder and spiritual leader of the Tunisian Islamic movement *Al-Nahda*. His writings about reason, *ijtihad*, democracy and public freedom are examined in detail. Ghannouchi is a product of a secular education. However, his knowledge of the Islamic faith grew after he became the leader of *Al-Nahda*.

HIS LIFE AND UPBRINGING

Ghannouchi was born in 1941 in the small village of Gabes in southeast Tunisia.[1] His origins were humble; in his own words: "I come from a religious household. My father was the only literate man in the village. He knew the Qur'an by heart and he led the people in prayer. He taught the children Qur'an for free" (Ghannouchi 2001: 16). His father was the imam and mufti of his village. Ghannouchi's upbringing emphasized religion; he memorized the Qur'an at an early age.

Ghannouchi's father tried his hand at trade, but failed and went back to farming. The whole family worked together to farm the land from early dawn until sunset, then

We would all head home at the end of the day and our daily dinner
was couscous that we would gladly devour. Then we would spend the
rest of the night weaving baskets, especially in winter. Tea was served
and we would all sing religious songs led by my mother's sweet voice.
(Ghannouchi 2001: 16–7).

In these early years, Ghannouchi's responsibility was to sell
the harvest. He recalled: "I would take the harvest to the
market to exchange for the few items that we did not produce
at home, like tea, sugar, salt and oil" (Ghannouchi 2001: 17).

During Ghannouchi's childhood, World War Two was
underway and Tunisia was seeking its independence from
France. His family was remote from Western influences.
However, Ghannouchi's little village was aware of the rise of
nationalistic fervor. The common custom of living with one's
extended family opened Ghannouchi's eyes to the political
mood of the country.

Ghannouchi was greatly influenced by his maternal uncle,
Bashir, who was part of the Tunisian nationalist movement.
He was an avid admirer of pan-Arabism as an ideology and
Gamal Abdel-Nasser of Egypt as an Arab leader. Through this
influence Ghannouchi became acutely aware of and attracted
to the Tunisian resistance movement against the French as
well as to Nasserism.

At the tender age of twelve, Ghannouchi witnessed a
horrifying and violent spectacle: After killing four resistance
fighters, the French troops displayed their bodies in the
marketplace for all to see. On returning home from school,
Ghannouchi witnessed this terrible scene and became at that
instant fully committed to his country's nationalist quest for
independence.

In that same year, he had to leave school to help his sick
father farm and harvest the land. All of Ghannouchi's brothers

had left for Tunis, some for work, others for education. After a year he was able to return to school. Until that point, he had attended a Western-style institution. However, upon resuming education, he went to a more religiously-inclined school run by al-Zaytouna.[2]

Meanwhile, the town of Gabes was becoming increasingly Westernized. Inevitably influenced by this trend, Ghannouchi began to feel alienated from his traditional and religious upbringing. Upon graduation, he discovered that with only an Arabic language education, it was impossible for him to pursue a college degree in Tunisia. In effect, at that time a Zaytouna education meant automatic exclusion from higher education because all local universities had adopted French as their language of instruction.

This was a major reason for Ghannouchi's departure for Egypt, but not the only one. His developing ideological stance also strongly influenced his desire to seek a college degree in that country. As with many Arab youths in the 1950s and 1960s, he considered Nasser to be an Arab hero. Nasser's support for Algeria's Ben Bella inspired Ghannouchi's pan-Arabism. In direct contrast to the policies of Tunisia's first president, Habib Bourguiba,[3] Nasser's policies and speeches supported the call for and commitment to Arab unity.

Furthermore, despite his Zaytouna education, Ghannouchi became distanced from Islam. He says:

I graduated from Zaytouna with no interest in Islam, except for whatever my father taught me. On the ideological side I was closer to doubt and rebellion against everything traditional. My mindset was a reflection of the teaching methods at Zaytouna. My education did not provide me with faith in Islam—it felt like we were in a museum in the Islamic jurisprudence classes. When I left campus, I felt that my

surroundings and modernity in the contemporary world had nothing
to do with Islam (as it was taught at al-Zaytouna).

(Ghannouchi 2001: 19)

Ghannouchi moved to Cairo[4] and, together with other
Tunisian students, was granted permission by Nasser to live
and study at Cairo University.[5] However, his admiration for
Nasserism began to fade when he saw the plight of Egyptians
under his rule. The big blow to his idealistic image of Nasser
came when he learned that Nasser had agreed to extradite the
Tunisian students to reinforce a more favorable relationship
with Bourguiba. Fleeing Egypt, Ghannouchi and the other
Tunisian students reached Syria, barely before the Tunisian
embassy caught them.

In Damascus, Ghannouchi became well versed in the
political mood of the *Mashreq*[6] (the Arab East) and was
introduced to the ongoing debate between Ba'athism,
Nasserism and the Islamic trend. Among these outlooks,
the definition of progress and development differed widely.
Ghannouchi was losing trust in the socialist/secular agenda
put forth by Arab leaders. While living in Egypt and Syria,
his Nasserist ideals became vague and ill-defined.

Ghannouchi was deeply moved by the variance between the
Mashreq's and the *Maghreb's* (the Arab West) understanding
of Arabism. In the *Mashreq*, Islam coexisted with several
religious minorities and pan-Arabism was used almost
synonymously with secularism. The pan-Arab view of Arab
unity drew on nationalism rather than religion. Its adherents
saw Arabism and the Islamist trend as mutually exclusive.
Thus, Egypt's Nasser espoused pan-Arabism and opposed
his local Islamic movement, the Muslim Brotherhood, in the
1950s and 1960s.

In the more homogeneous societies of the *Mahgreb*, the words Islam and Arab are used synonymously. In contrast to the *Mashreq*, pan-Arabism was not seen as an ideology opposed to Islam or in conflict with it.

By the third year of his education in Syria (1966), Ghannouchi abandoned leftist/Nasserist thought and became more involved in the Islamic trend (Tamimi 2000: 22).

After the academic year ended in June 1965, he embarked on a seven-month trip to Europe, visiting Turkey, Bulgaria, Yugoslavia, Austria, Germany, France, Belgium and Holland. Ghannouchi writes that he worked for three months in Germany in a commercial company that distributes goods to the Rhur region and that this gave him the chance to practise his German. In France, he harvested grapes; in Belgium he washed dishes in a restaurant; and in Holland he assisted a carpenter for a month and a half. Of all those countries, he felt most welcomed in Holland because he was invited by a family there during Christmas time (Ghannouchi 2001: 25).

Upon his return to Syria from this trip in 1966, Ghannouchi became increasingly persuaded by the Islamist arguments (Ghannouchi 2001: 26). He recalls:

I refused to join a certain group or party and in Syria I got to know the Muslim Brothers, the Liberation Party, the Sufists and the Salafis. I went to many *halaqas* (lectures), but I was most impressed by Sheikh Nasser al-Din al-Albani. He, may God rest his soul, wanted to liberate Islam from all myths. He introduced me to Ibn Taymiya and Ibn al-Qayim, and this has left an indelible mark on my thought.
(Ghannouchi 2001: 32)

During the 1967 war, Ghannouchi joined a demonstration in Damascus requesting arms to fight. The Syrian government gave the demonstrators Yugoslav weapons that were very ineffective, according to Ghannouchi (Ghannouchi 2001: 24–5).

After graduating from college, Ghannouchi was accepted on to the Philosophy of Education program at the Sorbonne in Paris in 1968 (Tamimi 2000: 23).

He was quickly confronted with many of the problems that Muslim immigrants face in the Western world, such as cultural differences, the inability to find *halal* food and so forth. Even though, while in Syria, Ghannouchi had already switched ideologically from Nasserism to Islam, his stay in France reinforced his attachment to Islam even further.

Ghannouchi was prevented from forming a political group in the Paris mosque. However, he joined a group of students who had formed an organization led by an Iranian student called Fakhry. He even helped Fakhry translate some of the now well-known Khomeini speeches from French to Arabic. Eventually, this group was ejected from the mosque (Ghannouchi 2001: 37–8). Also in 1968, Ghannouchi joined a *Tablighi* (proselytizing and missionary) group focused on the bitterness of poverty and helplessness of the foreign underclass in Paris. He turned from Islamic philosophy and thought to the practical mission of preaching, giving sermons and guiding the downtrodden (Ghannouchi 2001: 36).

In 1969 Ghannouchi went back to Tunisia for a visit. During this sojourn he became acquainted with the *tabligh/ da'wa*[7] members who later became the leaders of the Islamic Tendency Movement (MTI), which he founded. While in Tunisia, he dropped his plans to return to France and complete his degree.

Ghannouchi became active in Tunisian religious circles and, by 1973, had assembled a group of 40 followers. The *Tabligh* group then elected him as their leader. When Ghannouchi took the reins, he and his group began analyzing the Muslim Brotherhood movement in Egypt and Syria. Soon enough, the Tunisian regime under Bourguiba grew increasingly uncomfortable with Ghannouchi and his followers.

Ideologically, Ghannouchi tried to distance himself from the Muslim Brotherhood experience, developing the idea of "Tunisian specificity" (Tamimi 2000: 40–6). His main critique, though, was not of organizational issues, but focused on Sayid Qutb's[8] writings and their relevance to the Tunisian experience.

By 1978, discontent with Bourguiba's policies was rapidly escalating. At that point, Ghannouchi and his group were becoming increasingly political. He wrote:

> The workers' revolt, which was the apex of the leftist activism in Tunisia, had awakened us from our slumber and had alerted us to the importance and the social and economic ramifications of the problems the workers had been complaining of. Prior to that moment, we had been preoccupied with the issues of *da'wa* and *tabligh* and with pure intellectual debate.
>
> (Tamimi 2000: 50)

Thus, the *da'wa* nature of his group became more involved with issues that pertain to governance, economics and social justice. This preoccupation with social justice naturally evolved from the Muslim Brotherhood experience and Qutb's influential work, *Social Justice in Islam*.[9] The socioeconomic component of the Tunisian experience stimulated members of the Islamic Tendency Movement (MTI) to join hands with the leftists. In May 1980, Ghannouchi's movement orchestrated a 5000-member rally in support of Labor Day and farmers' rights (Tamimi 2000: 52).

Among the ideas and historical influences on Ghannouchi's life and leadership of the MTI (known in French as the *Movement Tendencie Islamique*) was the Iranian revolution. He was particularly impressed with the Iranian revolution's analysis of the conflict between the rich and the poor. Ghannouchi notes:

> Henceforth, our criticism of the state was no longer just religious or moral as in the past. It had become more profound. The rift between the regime and us had grown wider. From our point of view, the state identified with domestic and external oppressors; our own strategic choice was to identify with the oppressed. The state was for dictatorship and we were now for democracy.
>
> (Tamimi 2000: 54)

Ghannouchi was impressed with Khomeini's ability to unify the Iranian people in the face of the Shah and SAVAK (the Iranian secret police). He fully supported the Iranian revolution and published an article drawing comparisons between the Tunisian and the Iranian experiences.

The Iranian revolution set an example for other Muslim countries as well. Sudan was among the first to follow suit. The Sudanese revolution also left an indelible mark on Ghannouchi's ideas and leadership. Impressed with the Sudanese women's equal participation with men in the Islamic movement, Ghannouchi wrote an article about "Women in the Islamic Movement" (Tamimi: 57). His progressive stand gave support and inspiration to women, who began joining the cadres of MTI and actively participated with the men. Ghannouchi stresses that women's participation in MTI was necessary. It did not matter to him whether the women were veiled or unveiled, an issue that proves his progressiveness and belief that the MTI did not monopolize the faith or claim any religious superiority (Ghannouchi 2001: 71).

Due to an increase in members and the influence of both the Iranian revolution and Ghannouchi's visit to Sudan, the MTI began to assume a more formal shape. In 1979, the founding manifesto for MTI was written. Even though the MTI had not gone public, the Tunisian government was aware of its growth. Arrests of MTI members revealed the group's written manifesto to the government (Tamimi 2000: 58).

In the wake of the arrests, Ghannouchi held a meeting at which 70 percent of the members voted in favour of the group going public. At a press conference on June 6, 1981, Ghannouchi and his followers declared publicly the formation of the Islamic Tendency Movement (MTI) and announced that its manifesto was its statute, which meant that the movement had a political platform that would make it eligible to run as a political party (Tamimi 2000: 59).

The MTI manifesto, which allowed even communists to become members, caused Iranian leaders to denounce the Tunisian Islamists. In response, Ghannouchi said:

We saw that it did Islam no harm benefiting from the 'other', espousing and incorporating into our thought and strategy what we deemed useful and valuable such as the idea of democracy. Furthermore, we rejected the Iranian idea of 'exporting' the revolution and refused to accept that there was one single Islamic approach to change and reform.

Ghannouchi stresses the fact that there is no hierarchy in the Islamic faith and that no one can monopolize how the faith is interpreted and practised.[10]

Within a month of going public, Ghannouchi and 500 MTI members were imprisoned for four years (Tamimi 2000:

60). During his imprisonment, Ghannouchi memorized the Qur'an and read the works of Arab and Islamic liberals alike, including Tunsi, Muhammed Abdu and Afghani. He also read works in Islamic jurisprudence and was particularly impressed with Roger Geraudy's writing on women.

Informed by extensive reading and research while in prison, Ghannouchi made the first translation of Malik Bennabi's *Islam and Democracy* from French to Arabic (Tamimi 2000: 63).

Upon his release from prison in August 1984, Ghannouchi once again took up his studies and began working on his dissertation.[11] He also reclaimed his leadership of the MTI. At this point, the movement was changing from a reformist Islamic movement to one focused on domestic policies and the peculiarities of the Tunisian experience (Tamimi 2000: 69).

Despite being very careful, Ghannouchi was imprisoned again in 1987 on charges that he and his followers were violent Islamists who sought to overthrow the incumbent government. Ghannouchi and his followers were convicted and served periods varying from two to 22 years in prison. Ghannouchi himself was sentenced to life imprisonment, although President Bourguiba expressed the opinion that he deserved the death penalty.

In an effort to save Tunisia from civil strife, Zine El Abidine Ben Ali overthrew Bourguiba in 1987. President Ben Ali then released Ghannouchi and other MTI members. In 1988, Ben Ali supported Law Number 88–32, which allowed the creation of a multiparty system in Tunisia. In this new and encouraging political climate, Ghannouchi changed his group's name from MTI to *al-Nahda* (Renaissance) Party.[12]

In 1989, Ghannouchi submitted an application for party recognition to the government. In the meantime, MTI members ran for parliamentary elections as independents and proved themselves to be the strongest voice of opposition to the incumbent government. As a result, the government rejected *al-Nahda*'s application (Tamimi 2000: 70). Ghannouchi, however, was already feeling at odds with the government, which had awarded all parliamentary seats to the incumbent party.

Ghannouchi therefore decided to seek exile in London, England, where he continues to reside. His decision was timely; the other leaders and members of MTI were soon imprisoned in Tunisia. In exile, Ghannouchi continues to lead the party and over the years has authored many publications that have become central to Islamic governance, rulership and democratic practices.

REASON AND SCIENCE IN GHANNOUCHI'S THOUGHT

In 1969, when Ghannouchi left Paris for Tunisia, he and his elder brother stopped over in Spain and Algeria (Tamimi 2000: 28). Ghannouchi seized the opportunity to meet with the Algerian thinker and activist Malik Bennabi. Having read many of Bennabi's works, Ghannouchi was greatly impressed with his views. To him, Bennabi was "a pillar of Islamic thought and a revivalist of Ibn Khaldoun's Islamic rationalism" (Tamimi 2000: 31). Bennabi's writings always stressed the importance of reason and human analysis of religion.

Ghannouchi sees harmony between Islam and reason and believes that both should inform theology and law. He says:

> Both the Revelation and reason remain vital and efficient in the evolution of reality, so long as they remain intimate and interactive with it. With separation, reason expatiates in the deserts of abstraction, while legislation stagnates and corrodes. The dialogue between reason and Revelation on the one hand, and Revelation and reality on the other, is essential to the life of both reason and religion. Revelation's relation to reason is like that of the eye to light.

It is Ghannouchi's belief that reason and religion are co-dependent, that one cannot exist without the other.[13]

Ghannouchi views the ties between rationalism and faith through the concept of "rational religiosity". That is, the interpretation of religious textual sources is dependent on human reasoning and judgment and, therefore, rationality and religion are inseparable (Tamimi 2000: 42).

Tamimi comments on how Ghannouchi rejected *al-tadayyun al-taqlidi* (traditional religiosity) in favor of *al-tadyun al-'aqlani* (rational religiosity):[14] "Ghannouchi's group embarked on a process of *'aqlana* (rationalization), defined by Ghannouchi as the endeavor by a Muslim "to be in perpetual dynamism with his reality" (Tamimi 2000: 42).

Ghannouchi was impressed with Afghani, Kawakibi, Muhammed Abdu, and other scholars and liberal thinkers of the late nineteenth and early twentieth centuries. He was attracted to their analytic approach, inspired by the spirit of the Islamic texts, rather than the literal word of the texts.

The growing influence of writers such as Khayr el-Din al-Tunsi, Rifa'a al-Tahtawi and their contemporaries reflected a shift in the international balance of power. Western Europe was growing stronger as the Ottoman Empire was falling apart. Many scholars from Ottoman territories chose to travel to France, especially to obtain a military education. When scholars like Tahtawi joined the vibrant and highly-politicized student community in Paris, they began to rethink and reinterpret their faith to accommodate perceived European "modernity". They called for more liberal interpretations of the *nusus* (texts), that is, the Qur'an and the sunna.

Ghannouchi's admiration and promotion of the ethos of the texts over their literal words has caused some Tunisian Islamists to split from his movement.

Ghannouchi views the perceived conflict between Islam and reason as an inference drawn from the Euro-Christian experience (Tamimi 2000: 112). He takes a different approach to Qaradawi in considering the imposition of Enlightenment rationalism—the separation of reason from faith—on Muslim peoples. Emphasizing the role of modernization, justice and public freedom in a new Islamic democracy, he writes:[15]

The conflict in our history is not between faith and reason, or religion and freedom, and the people's will. All of those issues are included in the bases of the faith. The real revolutionary change and the true path to modernization do[es] not appertain to freeing the state, the public realm, and reason from faith. Rather, modernization and change pertain to freeing the faith, mind, humans, and the public realm from authoritarian states, thus allowing plurality, equality, democracy and the growth of civil societies.

(Ghannouchi article a: 3)

In another article, "Public Liberties in Islam," Ghannouchi says:

Freedom was bestowed on humanity (by God), to be able to act as guardians[16] of earth. However, human freedom and modernization are not attainable through reliance on reason alone ... Having to choose either faith in God and freedom, between reason, science, modernization, and freedom or faith: Europeans have limited the

applications of each. Islamic civilization is founded on a more inclusive
and holistic vision that combines faith and reason.

(Ghannouchi article b: 8–12)[17]

In Ghannouchi's view, "Enlightenment philosophy separates
between mind and spirit, spiritualism and materialism, and
religion and life. Its emphasis on the deification of reason
has created a materialistic understanding of the faith that
encouraged human instincts and drives without any control"
(Ghannouchi 1993: 96).

IJTIHAD AND TAJDID

The previous chapter on Qaradawi outlined his views on
ijtihad and *tajdid*. As principles in Islamic discourse, they
reflect the disposition of the author vis-à-vis traditional
(*taqlidi*) Islam and indicate his interest in renewing and reviving
sociopolitical Islamic discourse. Ghannouchi advocates
utilizing reason and logic in the reinterpretation of the texts
(the Qur'an and the sunna). This reinterpretation pertains to
al-dhaniyat, that is, issues left to human interpretation within
the spirit of the law found in the texts. These include matters
such as governance or the evolution of practices that pertain
to the adoption of new technologies.

Ghannouchi criticizes "traditional Tunisian religiosity"
because of its adherence to rigid interpretations that do not
allow for the free practice of *ijtihad*.[18]

In reaction to Iran's denunciation of the MTI, Ghannouchi
responded:

... we rejected the Iranian idea of 'exporting the revolution' and refused
to accept that there was one single Islamic approach to change and

reform. As far as we are concerned, the door of *ijtihad* remains open
and no one has the right to shut it. There is neither church nor a pope
in Islam that claims possession of the key to the Heavens.

(Tamimi 2000: 59)

Ghannouchi's thoughts about *ijtihad* are conceptualized as a
"vacuum" or a "space" in Islam where reasoning is allowed.
This space is "the distance that separates the Creator from
the created; it is a human space where man can exercise his
freedom and use his reason" (Tamimi 2000: 132).

Ghannouchi's conception of *ijtihad* goes hand in hand with
his notion of theoretical space, or *faraghat*. He argues that
the faith's claim to universality and eternalness is built on its
flexibility, and that adaptability is dependant on *ijtihad* and
the renewal of textual interpretations.[19]

Clearly, Ghannouchi perceives *ijtihad* as necessary for the
survival of the faith itself.

DEMOCRACY

The starting point for Ghannouchi's writings about democracy
is a strong relationship between Islam and politics. He cites
compelling evidence that links Islam as a faith to political life,
namely, 1) the historic precedence of life in Medina after the
Prophet's migration to it, and 2) an intrinsic agreement that
Islamic law handles private and public life.

According to Ghannouchi:

One of the good aspects of democracy is how it views humanity, an
issue that was of importance in the Enlightenment and Reformation
eras in Europe. However, the inability of those philosophies to:
1) balance between the material and the spiritual on the individual

level, 2) balance between individual and group rights, 3) balance between strong versus weak nations makes the Enlightenment philosophy incomplete. The Enlightenment era's separation of spirit versus reason and religion versus life: all of this resulted in the deification of reason so that a new religion was born. A religion that is built on materialism and individualism—a religion that has no place for reason.

(Ghannouchi article c: 11)[20]

Ghannouchi accepts Malik Bennabi's idea that democracy is a holistic concept, that is to say, democracy is more than a declaration that the people are sovereign, and more than an institutional system (Ghannouchi article c: 16). In this view, democracy relies heavily on the psychological and behavioral understanding of the people enacting it. It is more than just free elections and includes the education, socialization and security a people need in order to stride with confidence into the democratic experience. Bennabi writes: "[Democracy] is the generation of an attitude, and of objective and subjective responses and standards that collectively laid the foundations upon which democracy, prior to being stated in any constitution, stands in the conscience of the people" (Tamimi 2000: 66).

In agreement with Bennabi, Ghannouchi writes:

The problem is not in the democratic system: elections, parliament and majority … etc. but in Western philosophies that have separated the spirit and the body. Western philosophy ignored the spirit, and fought God, and struggled to replace Him with man.

(Ghannouchi article c: 32)

The similarity with Bennabi lies in Ghannouchi's admiration for democracy as a guiding principle, even though he views the Enlightenment era as a harbinger of extreme materialism and the annihilation of faith.

It is important at this juncture to mention that Ghannouchi is also influenced by Al-Imam al-Shatibi (as discussed in Chapter 2). Shatibi stressed the Islamic legal principle of *al-maqasid* (the end goals of Islamic law), which allows human interpretation of Islamic texts where necessary for the purposes of safeguarding public welfare.[21]

As mentioned earlier, Ghannouchi critiques Western political thought as: "the product of the grinding war, which took place in the West between reason and religion". Recalling the epic struggle that took place in Europe between reason and religion, Ghannouchi recognizes how the "despotic" authority of the Church eventually led to a loss of legitimacy. God's words were therefore replaced by man's.[22]

Ghannouchi perceives the legislative system and ethos as part of a democratic process that includes justice, Islamic law and public freedoms. He thinks that if each individual acts according to logic and reason instead of seeking out his/her own pleasures, then society as a whole would be just. As a result of his experience with the Iranian revolution,[23] he insists on the necessity of pluralism, especially as it relates to the interpretation of Islamic law. He says: "We saw that it did Islam no harm benefiting from 'the other', espousing and incorporating into our thought and strategy what we deemed useful and valuable, such as the idea of democracy" (Tamimi 2000: 59).

Ghannouchi is emphatically against the monopolization of religious interpretation and the utilization of those interpretations for worldly purposes. According to Tamimi, Ghannouchi endorses Islamic governance under the auspices of the *umma*, defined as a community based on faith.

The *umma* (Muslim community) should, ideally have the power to set up, advise, direct and dismiss the governor. The powers delegated by the *umma* to the government are limited, just enough to empower it to carry out the set of tasks pertaining to the implementation of certain aspects of sharia.

In other words, the Muslim community does not retire once a government is appointed; the government takes charge only of tasks that individuals and groups are incapable of carrying out. In this view, the Islamic political order is neither theocratic nor totalitarian because not only does the community concede very little power to the government, but also because sovereignty, within the framework of the supremacy of the text, lies with the Muslim community and not with the state (Tamimi 2000: 100).

Ghannouchi emphasizes the importance of the holistic nature of governance as well as the importance of accountability. He sees the mechanics of democracy as secondary, stressing instead the functionality and spirit of democracy rather than elections and institutions of democratization. He believes that Western democracy offers guidelines for the selection of leaders and political systems, and that it would be a mistake to reject it because of its deficiencies. A society based on inadequate law is preferable to the domination of tyrants—especially those claiming to speak for democracy (Ghannouchi article c: 33).

PUBLIC FREEDOM

Ghannouchi's contribution to contemporary Islamist thought is based on his study of public freedom. He believes that freedom is not merely a Western concept and rejects the common perception that Islam as a civilization does not advocate freedom. He writes:

> The reason that Islam is excluded in the discourse about freedom is that they (the West) conceive the individual as the center of the universe, while in Islam God is the center of the universe. Those opposing viewpoints could only be reconciled through re-examining Islamic law so that one does not have to choose between faith and freedom.
>
> (Ghannouchi article b: 1)

Ghannouchi notes the divisions that exist in the Western-Islamic discourse, for example, modern/traditional, and rational/irrational, and adds another—faith/freedom. In his view, the Western perspective of freedom stands in contradiction to faith.

However, Ghannouchi stresses the importance of freedom as a necessary foundation for democratic processes and a fundamental principle of liberty and civility in Islamic discourse. He believes that opposing tyranny is a necessity because tyranny is the worst enemy of the Islamic faith (Ghannouchi article b: 5).

Clarifying his interpretation of the word "freedom", Ghannouchi writes: "Freedom in the Arabic language is the opposite of slavery". Therefore, freedom in the Arabic context is a given, unless it is mentioned in opposition to slavery. Ghannouchi's comment is supported by historical precedence. He cites *al-Khalifa* 'Umar Ibn al-Khattab's saying: "Since when did you enslave people when their mothers have born them free?"[24] 'Umar uses the word "free" specifically as the opposite of slavery.

Ghannouchi further argues that, as a gift to humanity, freedom is the only tool that allows mankind guardianship of the earth (*istikhlaf*). Therefore, faith protects freedom rather than curbs it, to preserve the welfare of people. This notion of public welfare (*maslaha*) is well documented in Islamic legal texts, in which the basic principles of welfare are the protection of the faith, the self, the mind, posterity and wealth. References in Islamic law to justice, freedom, equality and propagation of mankind as parts of public welfare also exist. (Ghannouchi article b: 9).

According to Ghannouchi, the most important freedoms guarded by Islamic law are: 1) freedom of faith; 2) political freedom (the freedom to create political parties, freedom of the press, freedom to participate in elections as a candidate or as a voter, that is, governing should always take place with the people's consent; 3) social freedoms, such as justice, housing and transportation; and 4) freedoms for non-Muslims in a Muslim state, which should guarantee them the right to abide by their own laws in matters that pertain to family laws, food consumption, appearance, etc.[25]

Ghannouchi concludes:

> European revolutionary thought has created an impasse by forcing humanity to choose between science, rationality, progress and freedom on one hand, and faith on the other hand. Those choices are unwarranted, artificial and a result of a limited 'Western' experience. (Ghannouchi article b: 12)

The tenets of public freedom according to Ghannouchi are:

> 1) *Freedom of faith*, including a) equality, b) freedom to practice the faith and c) freedom of religious expression;
> 2) *Individual and human freedom*, regardless of faith, color or nationality in life or death; (Ghannouchi 1993: 52);

3) *Freedom of thought and expression*, because 'thinking is thought of as a religious duty (*fardh*)' (Ghannouchi 1993: 54);

4) *Economic freedom*, for example, the freedom to own property; and

5) *Social freedom*, including a) the freedom to work, b) the right to medical care, c) the protection and support of families, d) the right to education[26] and e) the right to social and economic support if the individual could not work.

(Ghannouchi 1993: 44–68)

Ghannouchi bases those rights on the Islamic legal principle of public welfare. He says: "Al-Shatibi writes that Islamic law ensures the pursuit of public welfare. Essential public welfare is clarified in the end goals of Islamic law by protecting the faith, the self, the mind, posterity and wealth" (Ghannouchi 1993: 39).

The bases for Islamic governance stem from the principle of the guardianship of the earth, because man is created proud, with intellect, with a free will and with responsibilities (Ghannouchi 1993: 97). Thus constitutionally, guardianship translates into two principles: 1) the primacy of Islamic law; and 2) the right to consultation (*shura*).[27]

CONCLUSION

Ghannouchi's shift from Nasserism to the Islamic trend is typical of his generation in the Middle East region. Abdel Nasser's speeches and actions created a stir in the 1950s and 1960s. However, his failure in the 1967 war, as well as his domestic policies, disenchanted the young generation of pan-Arabists, including Ghannouchi. His changing views are therefore a barometer of the political evolution of modern Middle Eastern societies.

Ghannouchi's travels to Egypt, Syria and Europe gave him a wide range of reference and an analytic approach to different ideologies. He is well aware of the dichotomies that riddle Western-Islamist discourse. His argument regarding freedom vis-à-vis faith reflects awareness of the Euro-Christian discussion about individual freedoms.

Ghannouchi praises the Enlightenment as the *agent provocateur* for change in the Muslim world. However, he criticizes one of the Enlightenment's basic tenets, which is the separation of reason from Revelation/faith.

Ghannouchi's well-rounded, cross-cultural understanding of the ideological dynamics of social/political change informs his moderate stance on issues that pertain to *ijtihad* and democracy. He is not as queasy about Western-style democracy as other Islamists, in that he is willing to recognize the ideological underpinnings of democracy as defined by the West.

How does Ghannouchi's understanding of public freedom and democracy affect the Muslim-Western discourse on modernity and democracy?[28]

5
Abdessalam Yassine: The Just Ruler

In this chapter the focus falls upon Abdessalam Yassine, founder of the Justice and Benevolence movement in Morocco. He has been put in a mental asylum and placed under house arrest for writing well-publicized letters to King Hassan and later to his son and successor, King Muhammad VI.

Yassine is a prolific author and his publications address topics such as democracy, reason, *ijtihad* and the concept of guardianship (rulership) in Muslim communities. As leaders of the Justice and Benevolence movement, he and his daughter, Nadia Yassine, continue to write, lecture and protest.

HIS LIFE AND UPBRINGING

Yassine was born in 1928. His father was a modest Berber peasant, and his family lineage is linked to *al-Ashraf*.[1] The family originally came from Sous in southern Morocco. Educated in Marrakech, Yassine was taught in a religious school where he memorized the Qur'an at an early age. His traditional education left him yearning for more knowledge and thus he read the works of European writers extensively (Shahin 1998: 193).

In 1956, Yassine began working as an education inspector; he continued to work in the field of education for 27 years

(Shahin 1998: 19). Dismayed by the corruption he saw in Morocco as a government employee, he became involved with the Batchouchiya Zawiya, a Sufi order, in 1965.

This period in Yassine's life was structured by the emotional framework of *da'wa* (proselytizing). The solace of living among the Sufis led to his later advocacy of *fitra* (natural instinct) as a basic necessity in Islam. Though deeply moved by the death of Al-Hajj al-Abbas, the ideas of many Batchouchiya members caused Yassine to leave the group. To him, they seemed more focused on superficial elements than on the spirit of the faith.

This break with the Batchouchiya marked Yassine's birth as a leader of his own pro-active movement. In 1974, he wrote an open letter to King Hassan that was printed as a 100-page book.[2] Yassine and his supporters distributed 1000 copies to intellectuals and public officials.

After reading the book (commonly described as "Yassine's suicide letter"), the king declared Yassine to be mentally unstable (Shahin 1998: 194). He was committed to a mental institution and then transferred to a prison. Yassine was held for three and a half years, without any due process of law. His friends spent 15 months in prison for collaborating with him. The authorities confiscated all distributed copies of the book, which was then censored and not republished until the beginning of this century, more than 25 years after the first edition.

In the second edition the book was divided into chapters, of which the first was a self-introduction and a summary of the purpose of the letter, focusing on the king's corruption and how to rectify it. In the second chapter Yassine gave advice to the king, accused his entourage, especially the intellectuals, of being dishonest and offered an alternative interpretation of political issues in Morocco. The third chapter addresses the effect of atheism on the younger generation and how distant Islam has become from being the central ethos of Moroccan society. Yassine again blames the intellectuals for neglecting their role as teachers and for making the hoarding of money their primary concern. In the fourth chapter, Yassine proposes a solution to Morocco's plight, outlining what should be done to rectify the ills of the society. Also in this chapter, Yassine identifies some ideologies, especially socialism, which he considered to be dangerous. He says that the army, the intellectuals and the economists could be the vanguard of Morocco's future. He emphasizes that if they are honest and hard working, Morocco would have a promising future.

In the final chapter, Yassine offers six points of advice to the king:

1. The king needs to legitimize his power.

2. The king needs to organize the military under the banner of true Islam.

3. An intellectual awakening abiding by the spirit of Islam should be encouraged.

4. A legislative body elected according to Islamic law should be created.

5. The economy should be based on Islamic principles of rights and duties and the state's responsibilities for public welfare.

6. A legitimate leader should be elected who would build a new Morocco, a country that would advance, with the efforts of its experts and the spirit of repentance, towards the common good.[3]

Following imprisonment, Yassine remained under house arrest. He considers the writing of the book, and the late 1970s in general, to be a period of "unorganized jihad". After his three-and-a-half-year prison term, he was forbidden from giving religious sermons until 1978.[4]

From 1979 and through the 1980s, Yassine and his followers tried to establish themselves politically through many channels. The first issue of *al-Jama'a* magazine appeared in 1979. *Al-Jama'a* initially appeared quarterly, then monthly. However, following publication of its sixteenth issue in 1985, it was banned for its critical and militant tone. According to Yassine, the authorities also banned the fifth, tenth and sixteenth issues of the magazine (Shahin 1998).[5]

Yassine refers to the period from the early 1980s to the present day as "organized jihad". In 1981, he formed a political group called Al-Jama'a al-Islamiya. In November of that year, he launched a new periodical called *al-Sabah (The Morning)*, which was banned after two days of publication and distribution of 7,000 copies (Shahin 1998: 194). In December, Yassine was arrested and sentenced to two years of imprisonment for allegedly creating public disorder.[6]

Yassine and his followers tried to gain legal recognition for the group formed in 1981, but were denied. Nevertheless, the group was still able to gain support and began developing an internal structure similar to that of the Muslim Brotherhood in Egypt.[7] In 1987, Yassine's movement became known as *al-'Adl wa al-Ihsan* (Justice and Benevolence). These two words proclaiming the goals of the movement,

were revealed in the Qur'an: "God commands justice, doing of good" [16:90] ... Justice is a popular demand and a divine command. It therefore must be achieved in all aspects of life. Benevolence is an educational program addressing the individual and the community. We thus combine two duties: The duty of the state and the duty of calling [to God].

(Shahin 1998: 195)

In December 1989, Yassine was put under house arrest. In January 1990, the authorities arrested members of the movement and officially dissolved it. Eight months later, in August 1990, Yassine was allowed to lead a Friday prayer which was his last public appearance until December 1995, when he also led a Friday prayer under the assumption that his house arrest had been lifted. However, his "assumption" was wrong and his house arrest continued until the year 2000.

In January 2000, Yassine sent another letter to the new king, King Muhammad VI, advising him to be just and fair towards his citizens and to correct the wrongs of his father. In February of that year, several of Yassine's family members were prevented from traveling to perform the pilgrimage. After his house arrest was lifted, Yassine led Friday public prayers on May 19, 2000.

While the authorities had relaxed their tight grip and Yassine was allowed more freedom to move, he was and still is kept under surveillance by the secret police. Yassine's wife, daughters and son were also dragged into the confrontation with the state, after being arrested in December 2000 for taking part in a rally for human rights in Morocco. Yassine and members of the Justice and Benevolence movement continue to be targeted and oppressed under the current Moroccan government.

REASON AND FAITH ACCORDING TO YASSINE

Abdessalam Yassine is a prolific writer. Throughout his books he discusses the role of reason in Islamic discourse. In his work *al-Ihsan* (Benevolence) Part II, he describes the place of reason in the Qur'an:

The kind of reason that is mentioned in the Qur'an and praised is not an atheist reason that judges only material things and does not know truth from falsehood. This mind (that is mentioned in the Qur'an), is the mind that thinks of creation, that is, of the necessity of a Creator for all that is felt and seen in the world. A second qualification of the mind mentioned in the Qur'an is that it deduces that there is a purpose for creation.

(Yassine 2000 II: 27)

Yassine criticizes the existing discourse about Muslim societies: "Why are we trapped in this binary prison: Advancement/ backwardness, modernity/traditionalism, and authenticity/ progressiveness! All of this craziness distances us away from faith and benevolence" (Yassine 2000 I: 366).

Yassine also criticizes "Western rationalism". He says: "The price of rationalism in the West is to free themselves of faith. It is as if there is no other way to utilize rationalism and analytic capacity, except by distancing oneself from faith" (Yassine 2000 I: 498).

Yassine's understanding and writing about the relationship between rationalism and faith are more strongly and clearly argued in his works: *The Muslim Mind on Trial* (2003) and *Winning the Modern World for Islam* (2000a).

Expressing the need to balance faith and reason, he writes:

The mind that believes in God and the Revelation suffers a loss of sight when it closes the eye of the common faculties, becomes incapable of learning from the cosmos, and abandons its tool to neglect and rust. It thereby fails to achieve the mastery of worldly life and sits idly in the company of the impotent slackers. That is a shortcoming and a lack of understanding the Revelation. God made the universe subservient to us and commanded us to move about the earth, to dwell in it and to compete and strive with earnest endeavor. That is impossible unless we strive to learn how to use this marvelous instrument called the mind. The believing mind is afflicted by paralysis and impotence in this world if it closes one of its eyes and turns away from competing in the arena of scientific and industrial endeavor, side by side with the common mind.

(Yassine 2003: 2)

Again, stressing the balance needed between faith and reason, he writes:

The Revelation did not eliminate the ordinary practical mind that manages the affairs of everyday life. On the contrary, it put that mind in charge of the common concerns of humanity.

The Revelation did not restrict the alert, inventive mind that manages and interacts with events, distinguishing the harmful from the beneficial and the sound opinion from the mistaken assessment. That is why God's Messenger (God bless him and give him peace) used to consult his Companions, seek their advice and mediate in their disputes in matters concerning warfare, travel, settlement and wealth distribution. He and they sought guidance from the Revelation, abiding by its text and spirit and exercising their judgment in its application to the extent of their ability, in accordance with the purpose to be fulfilled and in keeping with time and place.

(Yassine 2003: 15)

Yassine is quite aware of Enlightenment rationalism:

(T)he Enlightenment philosophy emerged from philosophical Copernicism, when Kant changed the established concepts. For him, "the mind is the center of existence around which everything revolves."

Today, the inherited Muslim mind still clings to its Islam. Yet it is confronted with the other mind, which took control of those minds that are ground in the mill of international culture, just as the malignant devil takes control of a person whom it renders insane.

The rebellious mind is now awake, strengthened by the might of inventions. Will the medicine of the Revelation and the remedial treatment of Prophecy be effective in curing it from its contaminating insanity?

(Yassine 2003: 40–1)

In Yassine's writing about empirical methodology and the exact sciences, he quotes a medieval Muslim scientist named Ibn al-Haitham,[8] then deduces: "The most important point is this: The statement we have read was fashioned by a Muslim mind that did not feel a need to reject religion in order to make progress" (Yassine 2003: 64).

Yassine draws an important distinction between philosophy and rationality: "Andalusia, whose light shone over Europe, was the cradle of geniuses in astronomy, mathematics and medicine, not that of the philosophers and their precursor, Ibn Rushd" (Yassine 2003: 65).

This distinction lies at the crux of the alleged divide between faith and reason. Often in Orientalist literature particular attention is paid to Ibn Rushd and Ibn Sina's philosophical works to demonstrate the rational/philosophical tendencies in Islamic literature. Islamic jurisprudence has been little studied, because it is allegedly faith-dependent. However, in this literature Orientalists have construed the relationship between faith and reason to be mutually exclusive, rendering it impervious to, or disinterested in, the application of reason or rationality.

However, Yassine points out:

The first Muslims did not recoil from seeking proof and exercising judgment. They did not neglect any of the functions of the descriptive, informative, empirical mind. On the contrary, they used them to confirm their faith that was established by the evidence of the Revelation. The evidence of the scientific mind served to substantiate the testimony of faith.

(Yassine 2003: 88)

In *Winning the Modern World for Islam*, Yassine links the rationality versus faith argument to the discourse on modernity.[9] According to Yassine, the Western interpretation of modernity is averse to faith. He says: "To be modern, it is supposed, means one must rebel against the sacred, against the divine. Ideological modernism owes it to itself to have as its goal disencumbering the way. This is rationalism's violent indictment of the irrational" (Yassine 2000a: 4).

Further on Yassine sees Islam specifically as a direct target of what he refers to as "critical ideology", because being critical means being opposed to everything that is deemed irrational.[10]

The historical watershed of colonization and its repercussions are also part of Yassine's discourse on modernity:

> In the physical absence of the former colonizer, the struggle goes on among us against Islam in the name of freedom of thought, of democratic pluralism outside of any Islamic norm, and of the right to be different—like the right to call oneself a Muslim without having the conviction. The ideals being proposed and imposed are those of atheist rationalism, materialist notions of progress and a secularism that looks down its nose at religion like some sort of allergy.
>
> (Yassine 2000a: 147–8)

Yassine says that Western calls for "freedom of thought" or "democratic pluralism" are tantamount to an insistence on "atheist rationalism" and "materialist progress". This point will be further elaborated on in the concluding chapter.

YASSINE'S VISION OF *SHURA* AND DEMOCRACY

Yassine's publications on democracy show that he links pluralism and democracy with enlightenment rationalism, which he refers to as "atheist rationalism", and modernity. Yassine's view of democracy is closely linked to current Middle East politics. For example, he cites Algeria as a case in which democracy was "put to death with enthusiastic pity, for fear that the enemies of democracy—those bearded fanatics and bizarrely costumed women—would commit an outrage" (Yassine 2000a: 156). Yassine criticizes the indigenous "secularist democrats" and insists that "a democrat should open himself democratically to the other and not impose his absolute, his singular notions on another" (Yassine 2000a: 157).

Yassine believes that the Western concept of democracy is "[b]y birth, freedom from every absolute except its own, an enemy to every ethic that differs from its own". He also criticizes the "Western" mindset:[11] To this mindset, any idea, any notion that departs from the secularist syllabus is the ramblings of a deranged brain" (Yassine 2000a: 157–8).

The imposition of democracy and the equating of it with the Islamic practice of *shura* (consultancy) is severely rejected in Yassine's writing. He says:

By transporting democracy in space and time, and by trying to draw parallels between democracy and *shura*, the only thing that has happened is the attempted smuggling of an exotic bird that is destined for certain death in a climate different from its own. The anachronism and climatic estrangement to which *shura* has been subjected to by comparing it with modern democracy are certain means for exiling *shura* to some ghetto of confusion and ambiguity.

(Yassine 2000a: 161)

The argument of Yassine and other Islamists about the discourse between East and West is stark: "Just as a mind formed in a secular school is amazed at Islam's "mixing" of the two spheres, we are amazed at the oddness of separating private from public life and the mosque from parliament" (Yassine 2000a: 160).

Yassine's definition of democracy is further elaborated in his book *al-Shura wa al Dimoqratiya (Shura and Democracy)*. He outlines nine conditions that make a political system democratic:

1. The existence of a nation state that unifies a people because of shared heritage, language, history, etc.;
2. The existence of a social contract that preserves the rights and duties of the people and the state, as indicated by Rousseau;
3. The active involvement of organizations and groups that represent civil society;
4. The recognition of certain individual rights like security, livelihood, and participation in the political system, etc.;
5. The sovereignty of the people;
6. A social contract that separates and balances powers in society (This measure is to ensure that the ruler has no absolute powers.);
7. The citizen's observance of the laws (There should be no exceptions, i.e. the laws should be respected and applied with no exceptions.);
8. Public freedoms such as the freedom to express oneself, freedom of the press, freedom of research and freedom of opposition; and
9. Respect for human rights and above all the respect of the right to access and know the political and economic state of affairs in a given country.

(Yassine 1996: 45–111)

Yassine's version of a democratic system is in many ways parallel to Western democratic systems, yet he is extremely cautious regarding the spirit that fathered democratic practices, that is, secularism or what he also refers to as "atheistic rationalism".

Yassine argues that Islamic jurisprudential thought lacks an adequate definition of a political system. He believes that there should be a new interpretation of the textual sources of Islamic *tajdid* (renewal) that would inform the creation of a modern Islamic state. Yassine rejects the "Other's philosophy" and he also rejects the "religious inheritance" (old religious interpretations), when it comes to his vision of the modern state. Pluralism, as Yassine interprets it, should stem from the fraternal bond in Islam, just as pluralism stems from the democracy of the "Other" (Yassine 2000 II: 156).

Despite his critiques, Yassine attempts to reconcile the concepts of *shura* and democracy. He writes that "Democratic forms and methods, applied with precaution and discernment, cannot harm *shura*; indeed, *shura* needs them to take effect in the modern world. Only the other face of democracy— the religion of secularism—is unacceptable" (Yassine 2000a: 164). Yassine confirms his admiration for certain aspects of democratic political systems. He says:

> In the democratic system, the balance of power owes everything to the existence of political and business organizations whose critical activity and rotation in power constitute the rhythm of political life. Public debate, the free expression of contrary opinion, as well as a diverse free press, aware of its responsibility, constitute the essential instruments to be borrowed from democracy. The organization of Islamic power has much to learn from the peaceful manner in which differences are dealt with in a democracy.
>
> (Yassine 2000a: 165)

While Yassine remains deeply suspicious of the cultural baggage that is attached to democratic practice, that is, secularism and "atheist rationalism", he champions the adoption of democracy as a political system.

IJTIHAD

As a principle, *ijtihad* is important because it necessitates the re-examination of the texts on issues that pertain to *mu'amalat* (the relationship between humans).[12] When Yassine and others call for *tajdid* (renewal) or *ijtihad* (reinterpretation of the texts), they consider them to be automatically open to life's necessary adjustments. Yassine is open to utilizing reason to resolve issues that are left open ended in the textual sources (the Qur'an and the sunna). He concurs that "God grants us the liberty to choose the best way to manage our affairs as a function of time and space" (Yassine 2000a: 162).

It is important to note, though, that Yassine's enthusiasm for change is curbed by his conviction that "[r]enewal could not be applied to *al-thabit* (the absolute) in God's laws. *Ijtihad* is needed for modern life—but we want to Islamize modernity and not modernize Islam" (Yassine 1994: 40).

Yassine considers knowledge as "holistic", that is, it helps to create a state, organize the economy, establish the principle of consultation (*shura*), and create a system for *ijtihad* for contemporary times and for different peoples (Yassine 1994: 202–3).

Yassine emphasizes the importance of scientific methodology in critical, observational and analytic thinking. He believes that it is necessary to, and a prerequisite for, changing the Muslim literal and emulative mind to an organized, rigorous and creative mind (Yassine 1994: 204). He also pays attention to the intellectuals who will carry out this mission. He says:

> The *mujtahideen* have to agree on their methodology for *ijtihad*, they have to comprehend that Islamic law has a known set of end goals (*maqasid*). Upholding the end goals of Islamic law and achieving them

is not only part of worship, but also a mechanism for advancement. We
need to analyze where there is no textual source or the consensus of
religious scholars (*ijma'*). We need to include contemporary elements
of societal behavior and social relations—if this could be achieved,
then Muslims would have achieved public welfare as dictated by God.
(Yassine 1994: 207–8)

Yassine states that *ijtihad* should not be monopolized by
al-Azhar, al-Zaytouna and al-Qarawiyyin graduates.[13]
Intellectuals from all walks of life should participate in
interpreting the Islamic textual sources (Yassine 1996: 75).

However, Yassine is also wary of two issues. First, he is
concerned about the intellectual's tendency to go against
the text on the pretext of using reason/intellect. According
to Yassine, "This would associate the intellectuals to the
Mu'tazalites,[14] who defied reason so that anything that
displeases the mind becomes ugly and anything that the mind
finds pleasurable becomes interesting. Such an idea would
have meant abandonment of Islamic Law" (Yassine 1996: 74).

Second, Yassine cautions that *ijtihad* should be handled
with extreme care and that only people who specialize in
Islamic law should delve into *ijtihad*. According to Yassine,
"Not anybody who holds a certificate qualifies to participate
in *ijtihad*, especially not the 'Orientalist Islamists'" (Yassine
1996: 73).

DIFFERENTIATING BETWEEN
KHILAFA (GUARDIANSHIP) AND KINGSHIP (*MULK*)

Yassine's outlook reflects his conflicts with King Hassan
and his sucessor, Muhammad VI. In forming his ideas on
governorship, he reflects on his native Morocco and suggests

an alternative model, the *khilafa* (guardianship) style of ruling. Yassine's writing includes many examples of his stress on the ideal type of governance. In defining this ideal type, he quotes historical precedents linking his model of governance with Islamic history. He says:

> In Ibn Sa'ad's writing he mentions that 'Umar Ibn al-Khattab asked his companion Salman: 'Am I a king or a *khalifa* (guardian) of the Muslims?' Salman responded: 'If you collected one dirham from Muslim territories and you misspent that money then you are a king and not a guardian.' 'Umar started crying. He feared the responsibility of taking any wrong decisions.
>
> In another incident 'Umar said: 'I do not know whether I am a king or a guardian, if I am a king that would sure be great.' A Muslim responded: 'There is a difference between the two forms of rulership.' 'Umar asked: What is it? The Muslim man responded: 'The guardian only takes his rightful belongings and he utilizes it in the best way possible and you do that (thank God).'
>
> (Yassine 2000b: 11)

Yassine clearly makes the historical argument that by Islamic precedence kingship was not a favored style of rule. On the contrary, being a king was synonymous with earthliness and tyranny. The distinction suggests an ideal form of governance reflecting the concept of *khilafa*, historically, the guardianship of the earth.

Yassine stresses the importance of the guardian role by citing yet another historical example.

> Many of the prophet's companions said: 'If 'Umar is offered the goods of this earth with all its splendor and beauty, if he is offered the best of its treasures, 'Umar will cross over all of this without getting his feet wet.'
>
> (Yassine 2000b: 20)

This parable means that as a guardian, even if 'Umar were offered infinite treasures, he would not misuse public property.

One of the most important historical precedents that Yassine cites to clarify the process of choosing a leader was relayed in the Prophet Muhammad's last words when he said:

Welcome, may God bless, preserve and support you. I ask you to abide by God's rules and I ask God to protect you. I was your messenger on His behalf. I ask that God's rules be held sovereign in all matters that pertain to His countries and peoples. I am now near my death, near the end, paradise. I ask you to bid yourselves and others who will join your faith, peace, after my death.

(Yassine, 2000b 28–9)

The prophet did not name a specific leader to follow him. He also did not specify or set any regulations for governance. Instead, he outlined the spirit of governorship: To abide by God's rules. He also wanted the Muslim people to stay in "peace" after his death. The great value of this speech lies in its non-specific nature. It addresses the ethos of ruling and governing, not the specificities and mechanics of ruling. Even though the prophet's choice would have been totally respected, he did not wish to create any divisions among the Muslim people after his death and therefore left the selection process of the leader open.

Yassine mentions this in conjunction with the proper selection of a leader according to Islamic mores and *sira*:[15] "The prophet died without appointing a ruler; he only specified that Abu Bakr should lead the prayers. Therefore, the companions deduced that Abu Bakr should rule"[16] (Yassine 2000b 28). The implication is that even though there were risks of internal fighting and divisions, the prophet preferred to entrust the decision making to the Muslims themselves.

Yassine cited this principle in the context of criticizing the political scene in Morocco: "Heredity rulership is the worst because it means the dismissal of the nation's opinion", thus alienating the people. To acquire a position of power in society through heredity is alien to Islam as a faith. "When a ruler puts his son in power or one of his kin, then they try to legitimize this by pushing the people to consent: This is an aggressive and bold act. Rulership, even the unborn is given the people's consent before they are born!" (Yassine 2000b: 69–71).

Yassine clearly differentiates between modern reality and the way things ought to be. Drawing a distinction in his discussion between guardianship and kingship, Yassine opposes the latter as a type of government and emphasizes the need for consultation and the consent of the Muslim peoples as the proper and ideal way for selecting a leader.

Yassine writes that when Abu Bakr was dying, he gave the people the choice to select their own leader, or to have him select a leader for them. The people agreed to have Abu Bakr choose a leader, because of his piety and knowledge. Yassine concludes that "[c]hoosing a leader for the people might sometimes aid stability, however, if it is abused then it is disastrous" (Yassine 2000b: 74–5).

Yassine focuses on this issue primarily because of his opposition to the incumbent Moroccan regime. However, his theoretical argument could apply to any part of the Muslim world. His focus on differentiating between the two types of governance, and his discussion of early Islam as a legal precedent for selecting a leader, both clarify and distinguish Yassine's political and religious position towards the responsibilities of leadership and his expectations from a "just" Islamic system of governing.

CONCLUSION

Yassine's experience as an education inspector has provided him with insight into the corruption of the incumbent government in Morocco. His membership and activity within the Batchouchiya also provided a strong impetus for creating "justice and benevolence". His differences with the Batchouchiya helped form and shape his independent political identity as a leader.

Unlike Ghannouchi, Yassine has been attached to the religious trend from his youth. He was not influenced by Nasserism and the wave of pan-Arabist thought that swept the Middle East in the 1950s and 1960s. However, the way he organized the Justice and Benevolence group, was influenced by the Muslim Brotherhood's movement (Shahin 1998).

The nature of governance in Morocco has served and continues to serve as a catalyst for Yassine's writing and his actions against the incumbent regime. His advocacy of justice is more reactionary than Qaradawi's and Ghannouchi's. His focus on the difference between the role of king vis-à-vis the role of guardian amplifies and expresses his reactions to the rule of King Hassan and that of King Mohammed VI.

Yassine's contribution in guardianship and kingship (*al-Khilafa wa al-mulk*) is an analysis of the precedence of the transfer of power in Islamic history. He also elaborates on the mores and rules that guide the behavior of the guardian and how this defines whether the ruler is a king or a guardian. By illustrating the means of assessing power and the way a ruler conducts himself after the process of selection has been finalized, Yassine clarifies his vision of the ideal government.

By emphasizing the difference between rationality and atheistic rationality, he shows his sensitivity to the dismissal of faith by Enlightenment rationality. Yassine's clear opposition to this mindset makes him very suspicious of Western democracy.

Nevertheless, Yassine strongly advocates the need to renew and reinterpret the faith within the confines of issues that are open to reinterpretation. He champions reinterpretation (*ijtihad*) and the end goals of Islamic law (*al-maqasid*) as principles that will guide the development of a just Islamic society. Even though he is ambivalent about Western democracy, his comparison between *shura* (consultancy) and democracy together with his elaboration on the nature of *khilafa* (guardianship) emphasize the moral code and ethos of a future Islamic state.

Does "guardianship" resemble some democratic practices? Is Yassine also an "anti-American Democrat"? (Center for Strategic and International Studies: Middle East Notes and Comments: *Anti-American Democrats by Haim Malka, Vol. 3, No. 4, April 2005.*) Those questions will be addressed in the final comparative chapter of this book.

6
Conclusion
Reason and Faith: The Islamists versus the "Stillborn God"

This chapter first compares and contrasts the ideas of the three Islamists, Qaradawi, Ghannouchi and Yassine about religion and reason; *ijtihad; wasatiya*, public freedom, *khilafa*; and democracy. Second, with these ideas in mind, we discuss reason and its relation to faith comparatively in Islamic writings and in Western liberal thought.

A COMPARATIVE LOOK AT QARADAWI, GHANNOUCHI, AND YASSINE

Religion and Reason

According to Qaradawi: "Belief to Muslims is not against reason or intellect" (Qaradawi 2000: 12).

In his writing, he agrees that scientific methodology does not tolerate any "claim without proof" and is also tolerant of opposing viewpoints concerning the interpretation of the faith (Qaradawi 2000: 115).

As Baker notes, Qaradawi stated in 1996: "For us science is religion and religion is science" (Baker 2003: 48).

If we examine Yassine's writings, we will find that he criticizes "Western" rationality because it depends largely on precluding faith, he writes: "It is as if there is no other way to utilize rationalism and analytic capacity except by distancing oneself from faith" (Yassinee 2000 I: 498).

Yassine draws on Ibn Haithem, an Arab-Muslim scientist to prove that: "The statement was fashioned by a Muslim mind that did not feel a need to reject religion in order to make progress" (Yassine 2003: 64).

Yassine stresses that, in early Islamic history, reason was used to affirm and examine the faith as well as contribute to research in sciences, mathematics, and medicine.

Ghannouchi, Qaradawi and Yassine generally concur. Ghannouchi stresses that reason and religion are co-dependent; that the existence of one depends on the other, that there is a "need of each for the other, for mutual rejuvenation" (Tamimi 2000: 31). Like Yassine and Qaradawi, Ghannouchi stresses that rationality is needed to understand and interpret the religion itself. Ghannouchi and his followers focused their efforts on the approach of *'aqlana* (rationalization), a continuous dynamic process that deals with everyday realities. In this process, religion and reason are constantly interacting and evolving, as opposed to the idea that religion is a fixed and stagnant understanding of life.

Ghannouchi is also critical of imposing Enlightenment rationalism on Islam, because in his view the "conflict" reflects the Euro-Christian experience not philosophical absolutes. The separation of reason from faith according to Ghannouchi is foreign to Islam. He argues therefore that the historical and cultural experience of Islam is more inclusive and holistic in combining faith and reason.

The three Islamists therefore concur that: 1) there is no conflict between reason and faith, and 2) faith and reason are complementary and in constant interaction. They also stress the fact that the Muslim historical experience is proof that faith and reason have coexisted harmoniously, stimulating advances in the sciences, mathematics and medicine in early Islamic history.

Ijtihad versus Taqlid

The question of whether to follow earlier interpretations of the faith (*taqlid*) versus whether to constantly analyze religious laws (*ijtihad*) in order to bring forth insight regarding new circumstances lies at the center of renewing the laws so that they can withstand change.

The religiously rigid have traditionally opposed *ijtihad* because it opens up the gates to liberal interpretations of the faith. Meanwhile, Islam encourages its adherents to use the mind, '*aql*, in analyzing the faith because its claim to universality requires flexibility in all issues that are not clearly outlawed in the textual sources.[1]

The works of Qaradawi, Yassine, and Ghannouchi seem to agree on the importance of *ijtihad*. Qaradawi insists that Islamic movements will never formulate a solid "rational political ideology" unless the movements start paying attention to the different branches of jurisprudence that exercise the use of reason and the progression of *ijtihad*. Qaradawi goes on to explain that the arguments in Islam nowadays are over negligible issues mainly because the "literalists" want to protect the faith by limiting human interpretations. This leads to the suffocation and death of the faith.

Furthermore, in advocating for *ijtihad*, Ghannouchi also strongly asserts that Islam does not have a single religious source of authority that interprets the faith. In his opinion, nobody in Islam holds the "keys to Heaven". *Ijtihad* in this perspective is not only a call to renew and reinterpret the faith; it is also a strong stance against allowing certain groups/leaders of Islamic movements to monopolize the faith. Ghannouchi agrees with Qaradawi that the faith's survival is dependent on its flexibility and its followers ability to engage in *ijtihad*.

Yassine's arguments appear to contain some internal contradictions in these matters. On one hand, he agrees with Ghannouchi and Qaradawi that no one institution or movement should monopolize *ijtihad*; intellectuals with different areas of specialization should all participate. On the other hand, Yassine also cautions that intellectuals could utilize reason/*ijtihad* to reject the Textual sources of Islamic law as did the *Mu'tazalites*. A second contradiction in Yassine's writing lies in his stress on the necessity of Islamic legal training before a person should delve into *ijtihad*. If only the credentialed qualify, the institutions of higher education would de facto monopolize *ijtihad*.

The three Islamic leaders agree that faith should be renewed and reinterpreted; however, they emphasize different constituencies and methods. For example: 1) Ghannouchi and Qaradawi agree that people from all walks of life should participate in reinterpreting the faith; however Yassine is less confident in the participation of religiously untrained intellectuals. 2) Ghannouchi and Qaradawi advocate change and renewal because they both think that without *ijtihad* the faith will die because of overprotection. Yassine is more protective of the faith, careful to specify who should contribute to renewing and reinterpreting the Islamic texts.

These three thinkers all agree in principle that reinterpreting the faith is a necessity; however they differ in defining who should engage in the exercise of *ijtihad*.

Wasatiya, Public Freedom and Khilafa

Even though the Islamic leaders discussed in this book share several similarities in their focus on the relationship between faith and reason, and on the importance of *ijtihad*, they stress different issues as their ideological priorities.

Qaradawi emphasizes *al-wasatiya*, which basically means that he does not go to any extremes when interpreting the faith. He is neither very liberal nor very conservative in explaining and adopting rules and regulations in Islamic law. The principle of "centrality"—*wasatiya*—is designed to send a political message not only to Qaradawi's followers but also to Islamic extremists. Qaradawi appeals to his followers by providing an alternative to orthodox/literalist interpretations of the faith.

Ghannouchi's work stresses "public freedom", which to him goes hand in hand with a liberal interpretation of Islamic law. His focus also links Islamic rulings and methods to contemporary political practices that deal with human rights and the importance of adopting an equitable framework for governorship.

Yassine's letters to Moroccan rulers and his theoretical writings all reflect his desire to change the status quo in Morocco to a more participatory form of government. Rulership (*khilafa*) to Yassine has its rules and regulations according to Islamic law and historical precedence. Yassine argues that contemporary forms of government in Morocco do not comply with the Islamic guidelines of rulership.

It is clear that the three Islamic thinkers view and express themselves as moderates in the Islamic-Western discourse on democracy and human rights. On the ideological level they all concur on theoretical elements that make up some of the cornerstones of Western liberal democracy, which leads us to the final and pivotal question: "What are their views on "democracy"? How are those views comparable with Western liberal democratization? How do we define Western liberal democracy? Is the definition of democracy a unilateral definition?

Democracy

Each of these authors has written extensively about democracy, a key issue in contemporary Islamist thought.

Qaradawi emphasizes the importance of a regime's accountability to its people; he also emphasizes the necessity of having a pluralistic system allowing a wide range of opinions to be heard. Even though Qaradawi is a Muslim Brother, his views are radically different from Banna's[2] rejection of a multi-party system.

Qaradawi also departs from Sayid Qutb's writing about *Hakimiyat Allah*—the sovereignty of God—when he defines the term to mean man's interpretation of how to respect and uphold God's laws. In different parts of the Muslim world, Qutb's ideas about the "sovereignty of God" have been taken literally. Unfortunately, not only have Qutb's words affected Muslim understanding of the role of religious laws, they have also influenced the West's perception of Islam as inimical to the idea of the "sovereignty of the people", a cornerstone in practising democracy.

Similarly, Ghannouchi's writing stresses the importance of government accountability. Ideological pluralism is another issue that Ghannouchi emphasizes; to him the example of Iran's attempts to export the 1979 revolution to other parts of the Muslim world is unpalatable. He underscores the relevance of different ideologies and different cultures that affect and influence the interpretation of Islamic mores. Iran, according to Ghannouchi, is trying to monopolize the faith and its followers.

Ghannouchi slightly differs from Qaradawi in the amount of attention he devotes to the importance of education and socialization as the formative blocks in practising democracy. He states that democracy is a holistic process; that people have to be conscious of what democracy is and practise the attitude of being democratic. Current democratic "reforms" in Iraq and Afghanistan are nothing more than the superficial installation of a democratic "system" or set of political structures. Ghannouchi argues that the people have to be imbued with the spirit of democracy before institutionalization takes place.

Yassine is very wary of differentiating between *shura* (consultancy), and democracy. Although Yassine writes about pluralism, people's sovereignty, justice and the separation of powers—all considered basal to democratic practice—he writes that democracy is "By birth, freedom from every absolute, except its own, an enemy to every ethic that differs from its own" (Yassine 2000a: 157).

Yassine stresses the difference between *shura* and democracy because he cannot accept what he calls the "atheist rationalism" underpinning Western liberal democratic models.

Qaradawi and Ghannouchi echo Yassine's concern about the theoretical and philosophical baggage that comes with Western liberal democracy. However, they are more tolerant in accepting the word democracy and its practise in Muslim societies.

To further contextualize and explicate the ideas of Qaradawi, Ghannouchi, and Yassine addressed in this book— rationalism, faith and democracy—it is useful to address the ways in which Western political and philosophical theorists view the relationship between faith and reason.

REASON, RATIONALISM AND
THE ROOTS OF LIBERAL DISCONTENT

In Foucault's "What is Enlightenment?" he discusses the tendency to confuse two concepts: the "Enlightenment" and "Humanism". He explains that the Enlightenment is a well defined "set of events" that took place in Europe and stresses its historical specificity (Rabinow 1984: 43). He defines "humanism" as a set of "conceptions of man borrowed from religion, science, or politics" (Rabinow 1984: 44). Foucault concludes that:

> I think that, just as we must free ourselves from the intellectual blackmail of being for or against Enlightenment we must escape from the historical and moral confusionism that mixes the theme of humanism with the question of the Enlightenment.
>
> (Rabinow 1984: 45)

Foucault's argument is relevant to the Islamist ideas analyzed here because he clearly identifies the rigidity of the Enlightenment ideology and its followers. This rigidity lies at the crux of the Islamists' fear and seeming rejection of democratization.

The Enlightenment focuses on secularization as a pre-requisite for modernity and democratization, that is, the ideal type of authority as Max Weber would phrase it. Contemporary moderate Islamists are wary of the Enlightenment philosophy's dichotomy and intolerance of differences.

Not all Western theorists have thought that the "Great Separation" as Mark Lilla refers to the faith/reason dichotomy in his 2007 book *The Stillborn God* is necessary to the existence of democracy. Even Jean Jacques Rousseau—the father of the French and American revolutions—was radical in his belief that religion plays an important public role in democratic political life. In Emile, he imagines the education of a young boy and the documentation of the boy's life by his mentor. Lilla notes: "The Tutor guides this education behind the scenes, much the way a puppeteer manipulates marionettes" (Lilla 2007: 116). In many ways, this imagery is reminiscent of the "Allegory of the Cave" in Plato's *Republic* in which the person being educated does not realize that he is being secretly indoctrinated. Although in Emile's case, it is a lot more subtle than in Plato's *Republic*.

Emile eventually needs to interact with society as a young man seeking courtship. It is then that Emile has to call on a code of mores to guide him in his relationships with others. Emile at that point in his life cannot rely only on his self knowledge and his individual experiences to guide him through social interactions. Emile's mentor, therefore, relays to him the story of the Savoyard vicar. The vicar's story is built on the beliefs that: "there is a creating will in the universe; that this will is intelligent, good and powerful; and that man is free" (Lilla 2007: 121). The vicar's ideas about the "creating will", and its intelligence and power, all relate the vicar's perception of God.

The morale of Emile and the vicar's story is that Rousseau was extremely aware of the outrage he could face by reintroducing faith into the public arena in Europe at that time. In fact, the publication still aroused rage in Europe so that his book was burned and he was forced to live the rest of his life in refuge. Lilla's depiction of the story of the vicar explains why Rousseau's ideas were so revolutionary: "The vicar's faith is not the Christian faith. But neither is it opposed to Christianity" (Lilla 2007: 126).

Distancing himself from the dogmatic understanding and practise of faith, the vicar stresses the universal role of human conscience. This is precisely why Orthodox Christians would feel threatened by his ideas because they are universal in nature (Lilla 2007: 128).

Rousseau ends the vicar's story by advising Emile to: "take up again the religion of your fathers. Follow it sincerely, since it is simple holy and can be made consistent with both morality and reason" (Lilla 2007: 130).

Rousseau's vicar is very close to the Islamists discussed in this book, in his emphasis on the need to be religious and to understand that faith can be "consistent with both morality and reason".

In fact, the rigid constructs and dichotomy between faith and reason, and also between liberal democratic practices and religious mores are critiqued by Rousseau, De Tocqueville and many contemporary political theorists, such as, for example, Mark Lilla and Cheryl Hall. Lilla shows that when the enlightenment philosophy broke away from the Church and its authority, the result was an absolute distancing of divine revelation from public policy. Lilla argues that this decisive blow to "political theology" was and continues to be a challenge in Western societies.[3]

Lilla criticizes the Western political-ideological fixations that result from the separation of politics and theology:

These [*stories*] are legends about the course of history, full of grand terms to describe the process supposedly at work—modernization, secularization, democratization, the "disenchantment of the world", "history of the story of liberty" and countless others. These are the fairy tales of our time.

Lilla writes that "*The Stillborn God* is not a fairy tale. It is a book about the fragility of our world, the world created by the intellectual rebellion against political theology in the West" (Lilla 2007: 6).

Furthermore, Lilla stresses the failure to recognize the political-theological connection in Western thought. He says that the separation of religion from politics depends on "self-restraint", and: "That we must rely on self-restraint should concern us. Our fragility is not institutional, it is intellectual" (Lilla 2007: 7–8).

Lilla's "great separation" between politics and theology is the very threat that so concerns even liberal Islamists like Ghannouchi, Qaradawi, and Yassine. Lilla points out not only that this rigid separation is relatively new in the West but also, and more importantly, that the founders of liberal democracy never intended for that great separation or dichotomy to happen. Rousseau's allegory of the vicar to substantiate his claim that the father of liberal democracy and one of the main "social contract" theorists was not for the rigidity of the current liberal intellectual milieu.

In agreement with Lilla, I also wish to emphasize that Rousseau's student and the father of the world's "ideal" liberal democracy (the United States), Alexis de Tocqueville, agreed with his mentor. In de Tocqueville's second essay on America, Part 1, chapter 4, he writes:

In my opinion, I doubt whether man can ever support at the same time complete religious independence and entire political freedom and am drawn to the thought that if a man is without faith, he must serve someone and if he is free, he must believe.

(Bevan 2003: 512)

De Tocqueville warns against the danger of abandoning faith because total equality between men also has the adverse effect of awakening "dangerous instincts ... It exposes their souls to an excessive love of material enjoyment" (Bevan 2003: 512). De Tocqueville believed that excessive equality must be controlled or checked by religion in a democratic society. In describing American religiosity, he wrote that they:

practise their religion without shame or weakness but one generally observes at the heart of their zeal something so calm, so methodical, and so calculated that the head rather than the heart leads them to the foot of the altar.

(Bevan 2003: 615)

Discussions and arguments about the public role of religion have continued into contemporary political thought, whether one refers to post-modernists or feminists. Looking even earlier on historically, the Romantic era in European thought gave us intellectuals like Nietzsche, Bergson, Sorel, Durkheim and Pareto. Contemporary examples of intellectuals who challenge the theoretical status-quo include Roxanne Euben, in her work *Enemy in the Mirror: Islamic Fundamentalism and the Limits of Modern Rationalism* (1999) and Jurgen Habermas, a student of the Frankfurt School. In his debate with Joseph Ratzinger (Pope Benedict XVI), Habermas argues that "secular knowledge cannot disregard and dismiss religion as 'irrational'" (Mc Neil 2006: 50– 1). It is interesting that in this debate, the Pope recognizes that: "The Islamic cultural sphere, too, is marked by similar tensions. There is a broad spectrum between the fanatical absolutism of a Bin Laden and attitudes that are open to a tolerant rationality" (Mc Neil 2006: 74). That is to say, the Pope recognizes the tolerant discourse of what I define as the liberal/moderate trend in modern Islamic thought.

The work of Cheryl Hall *The Trouble with Passion: Political Theory Beyond the Reign of Reason* (2005) exemplifies a feminist critique of the great divide between reason and passion. Hall establishes a connection between liberal theory and "Western political structures, processes, and cultures" and criticizes their influence on public life. The underlying argument of her book is that "passions" have a positive role to play in society. If this positive role is not recognized, she warns, there will be "the perpetuation of gender inequality in politics and the stifling of political innovation" (Hall 2005: 36).

Hence, after examining Rousseau, de Tocqueville, Foucault, Euben, Lilla, Habermas, and Hall, it would seem that there is agreement from different fields of study on the importance of religion in public life. Rousseau and de Tocqueville are of particular importance, since in many ways, they have theoretically laid the foundations of Western liberal democracy. As founders of liberal democratic theory, as emphasized in their works, they were careful not to exclude religion/faith from political realms—which constitutes my first critique of "rational/liberal" current political theory. This critique also undermines the argument that secularization is imperative to democratization. Therefore, Muslim societies do not have to abandon the public role of faith because, given Rousseau's and de Tocqueville's arguments, this dichotomy in politics is not called for in a democratic society. Accordingly, the link between secularization and democratization is frail, which brings the discussion of democratization to more profound assumptions about how we currently explicate the word.

Democracy and Its Paradigms

Theoretical explanations and definitions of democracy have been evasive especially in grounding democratic theory in causal explanations. Democratization theories have been unable to establish with any certainty either the causes of shifts to democratic systems in certain societies, or to establish a viable causal link that explains why certain societies are more successful in their democratic transition while others tend to fall back into old political practices.

The literature on democratization reflects this elusiveness. For example, Ian Shapiro writes:

> The scholarship in this area prompts the thought that the state of democratic theory is a bit like the state of Wyoming: large, windy and mainly empty. It reveals that we know something about some of the necessary conditions for some democratic transitions, but that there are numerous possible paths to democracy, and that we should not be looking for a single general theory—certainly not a predictive one.[4]
> (Shapiro 2003: 7)

Shapiro also comments on the lack of studies that link "cultural and institutional factors" to democratization. Shapiro argues that the perception of the "common good" determines democratic practise in society and therefore when it comes to determining or comparing democracies, this perception of the "common good" is "comparatively a thin one". As perceptions of the "common good" differ from one society to the other, so might definitions of democracy.

David Held confirms Shapiro's views in his thorough examination of democratic "models". Held comments on the difficulty of creating "democratic models":[5] "The history of democracy is often confusing, partly because this is still very much an active history, and partly because the issues are very complex" (Held 2006: 3). Exploring the variations in democratic theory, Held stresses the difficulty of theoretically defining democracy and its processes.

On a more positive note, democratization theorists have come to recognize two important elements in their analyses: 1) democratization is not a unilateral project;[6] 2) undue attention is given to elections as the critical signifier of democracy. Nevertheless, elections are not the hallmark of democracy because they are not representative of the majority's will all of the time, except in a "trivial fashion" (Dahl 1956: 131).

Elections and freedom of expression are in some states adopted as symbols of democratic practice without the state actually following up on other democratic practices, an issue that has been clearly addressed in Schmitter and Karl's article "What Democracy Is and Is Not" (Soe 2009: 38–44) where the authors refer to it as "electoralism". Marina Ottaway refers to "semi-authoritarian" states that go through the motions of electoral and liberalization processes without relinquishing control over the political system, that is: "they know how to play the democracy game and still retain control" (Soe 2009: 29).

Discussion of the current elusiveness of what democracy means does not diminish the value and practise of democracy itself. Rather, it is an attempt to clarify that in theory and practice democracy is still an experiment in progress. More theoretical rigor is needed before one takes a unilateral definition of democracy as a yard stick for Muslim nations and the world at large. Thus, as theoreticians, we know that we cannot derive grand theory about democracy and its practise. For this reason, claims about the concept's universality should be constantly checked by its theoretical and practical limitations. Democracy, like the concept of an Islamic state, is an idea that has been revived relatively recently at different points in time (Feldman 2008: 1).

Political Islam[7] and Democratization Theory

Contemporary literature points out the disconnect between views and interpretations of "political" Islam and democratization.

The Islamists examined in this book are considered by many to be "Islamic democrats" (Feldman 2004: 61) or as "anti-American Democrats" (Haim Malka 2005). Qaradawi, Ghannouchi, and Yassine exemplify "moderate" Islamists. The analysis of their work is an effort to engage the non-Arabic speaking world with their ideas and public personas.

The views of "political" Islamists differ significantly. In the first place, part of the literature recognizes politically active Islamists to be legitimate representatives of their societies. However, there is doubt as to the nature of the government the Islamists might instate once they are in power.[8]

Secondly, most of the literature falls into two categories: One group of analysts look at Islamic movements as variants of transitional democratic movements, and accept their legitimacy as true representatives of their peoples. These people include John Esposito, John Voll, Noah Feldman, and Emad Shahin.

Other writers are totally oblivious to the popularity of those movements and their leaders and therefore discredit the idea that they might be politically productive.

Martin Kramer points out the 1978 "watershed" in Middle Eastern studies because according to him "a stern

Columbia literature professor published a book: Edward Said's *Orientalism*." Kramer makes the argument that since *Orientalism*'s publication, the discourse on "political" Islam has become increasingly apologetic and "self-conscious" in its study of the region (Kramer 1997: 171). It is rather difficult to discern how Kramer's ideas would apply to contemporary literature about Islamic movements. In one of the extreme examples of literature on the topic, Harris writes that:

> The end of testosterone in the West alone will not culminate in the end of history, but it may well culminate in the end of the West. Testosterone still matters. Radical Islam knows this. Indeed, radical Islam represents a revolt of the unbridled alpha male within Islam itself. It is a return to the spirit of the original Arab band of brothers that toppled sedentary empires, and spread Islam through the Levant and across North Africa and into Spain. The fanaticism of militant young alpha males, bound together by the artificial tribe created by Islam, was an unbeatable weapon when it was first forged during the period of Arab Conquests and its revival today is the fundamental challenge to the survival of the rational actor.
>
> (Harris 2007: 272)

Harris exemplifies an extreme that underscores fears aroused by Samuel Huntington's "The Clash of Civilizations" and similar works.

Where is the "self-consciousness" that Kramer alleges was started by Said's *Orientalism*? The biases and dichotomies in studying all things Islamic, including Islamic political movements, is tainted with ideological and nationalist fervor that does not affect how researchers analyze, for example, the IRA. In dismissing the depth of the theoretical issues pertaining to rationalism and reason, Harris simplistically creates a dichotomy between "tribal fanaticism" and "rational man" (the Western man). He concludes: "In short, for reason to tolerate those who refuse to play by the rules of reason is nothing else but the suicide of reason" (Harris 2007: 278).

In agreement with Kramer, Huntington, and Pipes, Harris stresses that only reason, as exemplified by the Western liberal world, should be tolerated as essential to discourse.

Even though Harris focuses on the dichotomy between Islamic movements and the Western world, the terms he uses underscore my argument about the age-old perceived divergence between reason and faith and how profoundly they have affected contemporary comparative studies of democracy and its processes.

The deeply biased question addressed to Islamists is whether they would abandon faith for reason in pursuit of democracy. The bias is that by "reason" critics mean "Enlightenment rationalism", which categorically rejects any role for religion in political life.[9]

Lilla's "stillborn God"[10] lies at the heart of Islamists fears of accepting democratization as defined by "Enlightenment" enthusiasts. Qaradawi, Ghannouchi and Yassine recognize the good that democratization will bring to their societies but reject the liberal-enlightenment elements of the package. In retrospect, the fathers of Western liberal democratic theory never abandoned faith and its public role. Why is it then that this has become the quintessential dilemma in studying Islamic movements and Muslim political theory?

Feldman summarizes American and European policies towards aiding democracy in the Muslim world:[11] "If nothing changes, or if violent revolution comes, as it did in Iran, it will be because no one was willing to disrupt today's convenience for tomorrow's necessity" (Feldman 2003: 198).

It is more convenient to dismiss Islamist arguments as irrelevant and irrational than to dislodge the "Enlightenment" paradigm and its pious adherents.

As indicated above, democracy has many forms in theory and praxis. Anti-enlightenment Muslim democracies and their leaders constitute a variant interpretation of the ideal we all refer to as "democracy".

For democratization to take place in the Muslim world, the individual peoples have to define and formulate their unique visions of just governance.

Glossary

Analogical reasoning: In logic, it is a process of arguing from similarity in known respects to similarity in other respects.

Deists: Deists are adherents of Deism. In the philosophy of religion, Deism is the belief that reason and observation of the natural world, without the need for either faith or organized religion, can determine that a supreme being created the universe. Deists typically reject supernatural events such as prophecy and miracles, tending to assert that God has a plan for the universe that is not to be altered by intervention in the affairs of human life. Most deists see holy books as human interpretations rather than authoritative divine revelations. Deism became prominent during the seventeenth and eighteenth centuries, in the Age of Enlightenment. In time, deism influenced other religious beliefs. Many ideas of modern secularism were developed by deists.

Desideratum (plural – desiderata): This noun refers to something that is needed or wanted. Its origins lie in the mid seventeenth century. It comes from the Latin for 'something desired'.

Episteme: The accepted mode of acquiring and arranging knowledge in a given period. An episteme unites the various discourses (legal, scientific, and so on) and guarantees their coherence within an underlying structure of implicit assumptions about the status of knowledge. This word is derived from the Greek word for knowledge or science, which comes from the Greek verb "to know". Michel Foucault used the term *épistémè* in his work to mean the historical a priori that grounds knowledge and its discourses and thus represents the condition of their possibility within a particular epoch. In subsequent writings, he made it clear that several epistemes may co-exist and interact at the same time, being parts of various power-knowledge systems. Foucault's use of *épistémè* has been asserted as being similar to Thomas Kuhn's notion of a paradigm.

Egregious: This adjective is often used to denote that something is outstandingly bad; shocking. It was historically used to denote something remarkably good. The derogatory sense (late sixteenth century) probably arose as an ironical use.

Governorate: A governorate is an administrative division of a country. It is headed by a governor. English-speaking nations tend to call regions administered by governors either states, colonies, or provinces. The term governorate is often used in translation from non-English-speaking administrations. The most common usage is as a translation of the Arabic *Muhafazah*, rarely *Wilaya*. The term governorate is widely used in Arab countries to describe an administrative unit. Some governorates combine more than one *wilayah*; others closely follow traditional boundaries inherited from the Ottoman empire.

Hegemon: A leading or paramount power.

Jurisconsult: A noun that refers to an expert on law. The word originates from the Latin "jurisconsultus" and emerged in the early seventeenth century.

Occident: This term for the Western world comes from the Latin "occidens", meaning "sunset, west", and stands as a contrast to "the Orient". It can have multiple meanings depending on its context. For example, it can refer to the time period, the region or the social situation. Accordingly, the basic definition of what constitutes "the West" varies, expanding and contracting over time, in relation to various historical circumstances. In the contemporary political and cultural context, the Western World generally refers to the nations of the Americas, the European Union, Australia, New Zealand, Israel and South Africa.

Rasonieren: This word originated from the German language. Enlightenment occurs when man leaves his self-caused immaturity. Immaturity is the incapacity to use one's intelligence without the guidance of another. Such immaturity is self-caused if it is not caused by lack of intelligence, but by lack of determination and courage to use one's intelligence without being guided by another. Humanity will reach maturity when it is no longer required to obey any authority that demands "Don't think, just follow orders". But Kant distinguished between the public and the private uses of reason: "Reason must be free in its public use, and must be submissive in its private use. Man makes private use of reason when he is 'a cog in a machine', that is, when he has a role to play in society and jobs to do." To be a soldier, to have taxes to pay, to be a civil servant were the examples that Kant had given. Under those circumstances, man finds himself placed in a circumscribed situation. In these situations, there cannot be any free use of reason. But when one is reasoning only to use one's reason, when one is reasoning as a reasonable human being as a member of reasonable humanity (which is the meaning of the German word *rasonieren* as Kant used it), then the use of reason must be free and public.

Schema: A diagram, plan, or scheme. An underlying organizational pattern or structure; a conceptual framework.

Glossary of Arabic Terms

Ayah (plural: ayat): Verse from the Qur'an.

Da'wa: The word refers to the Islamic call. It denotes preaching of Islam. It means literally "issuing a summons" or "making an invitation". A Muslim who practices *da'wa* is one who invites people to the faith, to the prayer or to Islamic life

Da'iya: Every Muslim is a *da'iya*, that is, one who proselytizes—a missionary. *Da'wa* cannot be given up or be a part-time occupation; it must become the life a Muslim lives.

Dhaniyat (singular: Dhaniy): In Islamic legal thought, this means doubtful issues. That is, an issue that: (a) is open to debate and (b) is not clearly ruled as a forbidden or favored act in Islamic law.

Fiqh/Fuqaha: Fiqh is the origin of the noun Fuqaha. *Fiqh* is the process of inferring Islamic law from the Qur'an and the *sunna*. The *fuqaha*, therefore are the legal scholars who perform such a task.

Fitra: is an Arabic word meaning "disposition", "nature", "constitution" or "instinct". In a mystical context, it can connote intuition or insight. According to Islamic theology, human beings are born with an innate knowledge of *tawhid*, which is encapsulated in the *fitra* along with intelligence and all other attributes that embody what it is to be human. It is for this reason that some Muslims prefer to refer to those who embrace Islam as reverts rather than converts, as it is believed they are returning to a perceived pure state.

Hadith (plural: Ahadith): The words spoken by the Prophet that were reported by his companions. The *hadith* is an integral part of Islamic law and is second in importance to the Qur'an.

Hasan: The origin of words like *istihsan*, *ahsan*, *muhsin*. It means good or beneficial.

Ijma': The consent of legal scholars concerning a certain issues. It is considered to be a source of Islamic law.

Ijtihad: Generally means making an effort; however, in the Islamic legal context it means mentally exerting an effort in interpreting legal edicts.

Imam: The role of Imam is an Islamic leadership position, often the worship leader of a mosque and the Muslim community. The *imam* is the one who leads Islamic worship services. The community often turns to the mosque *imam* if it has a religious question. But the Sunni branch of Islam, to which approximately 90 percent of Muslims belong, does not have a clergy and therefore an *imam* is not a clerical position like that of a Christian priest. In the Shi'i branch of Islam, the concept of an *imam* occupies a much more central religious position.

Istihsan: Its origin is *hasin*. A legal principle invoked as a general guideline in Muslim legal thought.

Istikhlaf: Guardianship of the earth.

Istishab: A legal principle invoked to maintain a certain practice, until the practice is repealed by a more accurate explanation of the law.

Istislah: A legal principle that applies public good or public welfare as a guideline for legislating Islamic law.

Khalifa (The anglicized version is Caliph): Historically, the leader of the Muslim *umma*.

Khilafah: In theological terms, humanity is the follower and caretaker of the Earth, after God. Therefore, each individual is *khilafat Allah fi al-ard* (God's vice-regent on Earth).

Madhab (plural: Madhahib): A legal school of law. The main four Sunni *madhahib* are: *Maliki, Hanafi, Shaf'i* and *Hanbali*. The Shi'i main legal school of law is *Ja'fari*.

Maghreb: The Arab west.

Mashreq: The Arab east.

Al-Maqasid: The end goals of Islamic law. The spirit of the law and its guiding principles.

Mashayekh (singular: sheikh): Muslim preachers .

Maslaha (plural: Masalih): Public welfare or the public good, sought by practising *istislah* according to Islamic law. In Islamic legal thought, the public good is qualified according to the Qur'an and the *sunna*.

Mufti: A mufti is a Sunni Islamic scholar who is an interpreter or expounder of Islamic law (*sharia*). A *mufti* will generally go through a rigorous course of study and must fulfill eight conditions set by scholars in order that he may be able to issue verdicts (fataawa).

Mujtahid: The origin of the word is *juhd*. *Mujtahid* is a Muslim jurisprudent who is able to extrapolate reasonable judgments on different legal issues.

Mu'tazalites: Followers of this line of theological thought urge humans to rationally try to understand the universe. *Mu'tazili* theology originated in Basra, Iraq, in the eighth century following a theological dispute. Its followers were labelled *Mu'tazili*. Later on, they called themselves *ahl al-tawhid wa al-'adl* (People of Divine unity and Justice). Although *mu'tazilis* later relied on logic and different aspects of early Islamic, Greek and Hellenic philosophy, the truths of Islam were their starting point and ultimate reference.

Al-Nass (plural: Al-Nusus): The text or scriptures, that is to say, the Quran and the *hadith*.

Qat'yiat (singular: qat'iy): The word is the opposite of *dhaniy*, which in *fiqh* means that the issue at hand is clearly addressed in the textual sources (*al-nusus*).

Al-Qiyas: A method used in Muslim law to extrapolate legal reasoning by analogy. For example, if drinking alcohol is prohibited because it obscures rational behavior, therefore narcotics are prohibited as well.

Salaha: The origin of *istislah*, *al-aslah*, and *maslaha*. It means the good, the beneficial, the useful.

Al-Sharia: The canonical revealed Islamic law that is found in the Qur'an, the *sunna*, the consensus of the legal scholars (*ijma'*) and from their use of analogical reasoning (*qiyas*).

Sira: The biography of the Prophet, that is, the entirety of the Prophet Muhammad's acts and sayings.

Sunna: The Prophet Muhammad's acts and sayings that were recorded by his followers as part of his customary and relatively binding practice.

Tajdid: Literally means "renewal" and can also refer to the reinterpretation and renewal of Islamic law.

'Ulama: (plural: 'alim): Religious scholars.

Umma: The community of Muslims, that is to say, the totality of all Muslims. It comes from a word that simply means "people". The term has been crucial to the Muslim understanding of unity.

'Urf: Local customs. In legal Islamic thought, some scholars agreed that local customs should be incorporated in the body of the law.

Usul al-Fiqh: The foundations of Muslim law. According to the Sunnis these are the Qur'an, *sunna*, the consensus of religious scholars and their analogical reasoning.

Al-Wasat/Wasatiya: The interpretation of religious texts liberally, that is, not too loosely or too rigidly as to stray away from the spirit of the law. *Wasat* in Arabic literally means "Center", so for a religious scholar it means to be centered in one's interpretation of Islamic law. It also connotes moderation which is emphasized and praised in the texts.

Notes

Chapter 1

1. Gellner points out that "When dealing with serious matters, when human lives and welfare are at stake, when major resources are being committed, the only kind of knowledge which may legitimately be used and invoked is that which satisfies the criteria of Enlightenment philosophy" (1992: 92). He also ardently concludes his book: "The notion of a Revelation favoring and endorsing its own source, reconfirming itself by a blatantly circular argument, is incompatible with that very cognitive ethic which, for all its emotional thinness, I find at the center of my identity" (1992: 96).

2. Islamic activists and populist Islamists are used interchangeably in this study. The reason for using them interchangeably is that populist Islamists qualifies the nature of the means used by the activists to get from point A to point B regarding the call for systemic changes, i.e. Islamic activists could range from violent to non-violent in their means to change public policy. Therefore, qualifying Islamic activism with "populism" indicates that the Islamic activists are non-violent, otherwise they would not be "populist".

3. By liberal/moderate I mean a non-literal perception of Islamic laws when it comes to what is called "doubtful" (*al-dhaniy*) in Islamic law, i.e. issues that have not been addressed in detail in the scriptures, thus allowing room for human interpretation.

4. Euben captures this: "The pleasant trope of 'conversation' must be invoked in the study of Islamic fundamentalism with caution, for in a postcolonial world such 'dialogues' across culture often take place under conditions of radical inequality among and between regions, economies, and cultures" (Euben 1999: 13).

5. Voltaire, *Candide* 1759, and *Micromegas* 1752.
6. Both quotes are from Mabro (1996: 54–55).
7. Mabro 1996: 74.
8. Winston Davis's article "Religion and Development: Weber and East Asia Experience", is part of Myron Wiener's and Samuel Huntington's edited "Understanding Political Development" (1987).
9. "I wonder whether we may not envisage modernity rather as an attitude than as a period of history. And by attitude, I mean a mode of relating to contemporary reality; a voluntary choice made by certain people; in the end, a way of thinking and feeling; a way, too of acting and behaving that at one and the same time marks a relation of belonging and presents itself as a task" (Foucault 1984: 39).

Chapter 2

1. Shatibi's date of birth is not certain but it is thought that he was born before 1318 (Abu al-Ajfan,1984: 32).
2. I will discuss this at length in the following section.
3. The end goals of *sharia* (*al-maqasid*) are five: Preservation of: 1) religion; 2) life; 3) lineage; 4) intellect; and 5) property. However, preserving those five elements is part and parcel of the more encompassing principle of public welfare (*maslaha*) in Islamic law.

Chapter 3

1. *Fiqh* is the process of inferring Islamic law from the Qur'an and Hadith (Prophet Muhammed's sayings).
2. Also referred to commonly in Islamic legal circles as al-Maqasid, which means the spirit of the law and its guiding principles, rather than its literal interpretation.
3. This system is also known as *madrasa* in Pakistan as well as other parts of the Muslim world. The products of such an education gave the Muslim world and Egypt, people as divergent as (a) Taha

Hussein, a professor of Arabic literature who graduated from the Sorbonne with a PhD, a secularist ideologue and a minister of education at one point, and (b) Qaradawi, a respected religious scholar who graduated from al-Azhar and a politically active Islamic leader in the modern Arab/Muslim world.

4. Hassan al-Banna founded the Muslim Brotherhood Movement in 1928 in Ismailia, Egypt.

5. Sheikh Sha'rawi is an "Egyptian Islamic cleric who delivered his religious messages by means of audiocassettes, videotapes, books, and especially his popular weekly lectures on television. From 1976 to 1978 he served as the country's minister of religious endowments" (*Encyclopedia Britannica Online*).

6. Those allegations were challenged by al-Banna in his last book *Al-Qawl al-Fasil*, which is still not circulated to this day.

7. Qaradawi says that al-Banna was still alive after he was shot; however, on the king's orders doctors were not allowed to administer a blood transfusion that would have saved his life (Qaradawi 2002: 332).

8. Plural for sheikh, or Muslim preacher.

9. One of the sarcastic and humorous pieces of poetry that the brothers created while they were imprisoned goes as follows:

> Why and why what did we do?
> I was sitting in my house, then those ghosts came in,
> they searched me and said you are a bandit, you are accused,
> when I asked why they responded: you are a brother, we found the Qur'an in your house,
> and religious teaching and prayer beads, and you have a beard too.
> Answer why? You pray without police permission and fast on Monday without a permit,
> you're always cautious for sunrise prayers and you pray upon the prophet Muhammed.
> Why and why? (Qaradawi 2002: 367)

10. His PhD title was "The Effect of Alms-Giving on Social Problems" (Qaradawi website—www.qaradawi.net/site/topics/index.asp?cu_no=2&temp_type=44—accessed October 20, 2010.)

11. *Ijtihad* is the use of human reason to deduce laws and regulations in line with the spirit and principles of Islam.

12. *Fiqh al-Sunan* is Islamic jurisprudence that is based on the verified Sunna—the words and deeds of Prophet Mohammed.

13. Stagnation, not renewing or reinterpreting the faith.

14. *Dhahiriya* is "A school of law which never gained a significant acceptance and is now extinct. It was begun by disciples of Dawud ibn Khalaf al-Isfahani, called al-Zahiri (the literalist). He had been himself a disciple of al-Shafi'i but he rejected completely the doctrine of analogy (*qiyas*), and the opinions of any but the closest of the Companions, and insisted upon a strictly literal interpretation of the Qur'an and the Sunna. The objection to analogy went so far as to even forbid searching for the reasons for a religious law (Glasse 1989: 430).

15. Centrist, meaning *al-wasatiya*.

16. *Fiqh al-muwazana* is the use of human interpretation and judgment in deciding between two necessary evils. For example, if a man is dehydrated in the desert and the only thing he could find to drink was wine, should he leave it because alcohol is forbidden in Islamic law? According to *fiqh al-muwazana*, his alcohol consumption under such circumstance is fine because human life is at stake and therefore his survival becomes more important than observing the legal code due to his dire circumstance.

17. Taking public welfare into account when making legal decisions under Islamic laws, which also entails the appreciation of cultural and norm differences amongst Muslim societies.

18. By democracy here I mean the basic Western-style liberal-democracy, that is, a political order that has a multiparty system, has a fair electoral process, is built on checks and balances of internal political organizations, observes relative political freedom, and is relatively accountable to the people.

19. Shura is the taking into account of the opinion of others when considering a complex issue, particularly when it also pertains to public policy.

20. The term "anti-American Democrat" was coined by Haim Malka (Center for Strategic and International Studies: Middle East Notes

and Comments: *Anti-American Democrats by Haim Malka, Vol. 3, No. 4, April 2005.*)

Chapter 4

1. Ghannouchi's biographical information relies on *Min Tajrubat al-Haraka al-Islamiya fi Tunis (The Experience of the Islamic Movement in Tunisia)* 2001, and on Azzam Tamimi's *Rachid Ghannouchi: A Democrat within Islamism* 2001.
2. Zaytouna is one of the oldest Islamic higher education establishments in the Muslim world.
3. Tunisia's first president before Ghannouchi went into exile. He ruled Tunisia during 1957–87.
4. He moved in 1964 (Ghannouchi 2001: 21).
5. Ghannouchi was accepted in the Faculty of Agriculture at Cairo University where he stayed for only three months (Ghannouchi 2001: 21).
6. North Africans (Tunisians, Moroccans and Algerians) consider themselves the Arab peoples of the West (al-Maghrib Al-'Arabi) and they consider Egypt and the Arab countries East of Egypt as the Arab peoples of the East (al-Mashriq Al-'Arabi).
7. Tabligh and *da'wa* is basically to proselytize and act as a missionary of the Islamic faith.
8. A Muslim Brother ideologue that was referred to in chapter two.
9. First published in 1949.
10. "As far as we are concerned, the door of *ijtihad* remains open and no one has the right to shut it. There is neither church nor a pope in Islam that claims possession of the key to the Heavens" (Tamimi 2000: 59).
11. Ghannouchi also got his MA from the school of Islamic Law, for his research: "Destiny in Ibn Taymiya's Thought" (2001: 45).
12. Law No. 88–32 did not allow for the creation of a party that had a religious platform; therefore, Ghannouchi changed the name of the Islamic Tendency Movement to something more secular.
13. "Neither may exist without the other. Such is Islamic rationality; it has as its foundation stone the principle of recognition of the

dualism of reason and the Revelation, and the insistence upon the need of each for the other, for mutual rejuvenation" (Tamimi 2000: 31).

14. "The debate within Ghannouchi's group included an endeavor to revive what was referred to as *al-turath al-Islami al-'aqlani* (the Islamic legacy of rationality). The need was felt, as part of the attempt to counter *al-tadayyun at-taqlidi at-Tunsi* (traditional Tunisian religiosity), to restore respect for *al-mu'tazilah* approach to interpreting the Islamic text. Based on the belief that human reason harmonizes with the Revelation, the *mu'tazilah* approach was deemed more conducive to the group's objective of shaking the foundation of *taqlid* (imitation)" (Tamimi 2000: 42).

15. Upon meeting Rachid Ghannouchi in London on July 5, 2004, he gave me a number of his articles (all unpublished). This article, entitled "Is Secularism an Antagonistic Philosophy or a Philosophy of Modernization and Freedom", is one of them. The article, he stressed, was a rebuttal of what was published in Azzam Tamimi's book about him (2000). For reference purposes this will be referred to as article a.

16. Guardianship, or *istikhlaf* in Arabic, is commonly used to refer to the role of mankind in Islamic discourse. It has been misleadingly translated into vice-regency. However, vice-regency connotes that the sovereign is a child, absent, or incapacitated. Therefore, the translation is inadequate since God in Islamic discourse is not a child nor is He incapacitated. Thus, the translation of *istikhlaf* should be "the guardianship of earth", not vice-regency.

17. A second article that is unpublished is entitled "Public Freedom in Islam", which I will refer to as article b.

18. The "predominance of imitation and shortage of *ijtihad* during what he describes as the era of stagnation in the history of Tunisia" (Tamimi 2000: 41).

19. "If Islam is the final divine Revelation to humanity, [Ghannouchi] argues, it is only appropriate that no fixed prescriptions are given for matters that are of a changing nature. By virtue of such *murunah* (flexibility), and thanks to the existence of *faraghat* (spaces) whereby Muslims can exercise their *ijtihad* to devise

suitable solutions for emerging problems, Islam is said to be fit for all times and places" (Tamimi 2000: 188).

20. Ghannouchi article entitled "The Basic Principles of Democracy and The Roots of Islamic Governance" (unpublished), which will be referred to as article c.

21. Tamimi mentions this in his work on Ghannouchi (p. 91). However, Tamimi claims that Shatibi "founded" *ilm al-maqasid*, and it is important to note that the principle was born with the faith, long before Shatibi wrote about it, i.e. it was always a principle that was utilized by the four guided caliphs, especially 'Umar. The principle was written about first by Shaf'i because he was the first to write in the field of *fiqh* (Islamic jurisprudence). However, the two leaders of the sunni schools that preceded Shaf'i (Abu Malik and Abu Hanifa) both utilized the principle a lot. Therefore, Shatibi was the main theoretician who studied and explained the principle at length, but he definitely was not the founder. (Abdelkader 2000).

22. "It is the product of the conflict between two antagonists. There was, on the one hand, the struggle for freedom, self-determination and the right to enjoy the goodness of this world on the basis of the centrality of man in the universe and the absolute ability of reason to understand and explain the universe and to organize life. On the other hand, there was the church and its despotic authority, which it exercised for many centuries of darkness, backwardness and oppression. Reason and science eventually won the war. As a result the people recovered their rights and rid themselves of the church's control over man's mind and conscience and over the organization of life. In the end, natural law replaced God's Revelation as the philosophical basis for legislation" (Tamimi 2000: 96).

23. Two leaders of Iran have ridiculed Ghannouchi and his movement (MTI) because the MTI was too pluralistic by accepting the political participation of socialist parties, as part of the MTI's manifesto/platform.

24. The context of 'Umar's words is important. Upon conquering Egypt, 'Amr Ibn al-'As slapped an Egyptian Jew, so when 'Umar heard the story, he responded with the famous words mentioned above.

25. Ghannouchi wrote a book on this matter, *National Rights: the Non-Muslims' Rights in a Muslim Society* (Ghannouchi, 1993).
26. Ghannouchi writes: "Islam is the first faith to require education. Education is a duty for male and female Muslims" (Ghannouchi 1993: 63).
27. Consultation in Islamic legal/political thought asserts that the ruled have the right to consult and advise the ruling body or guardian.
28. The concluding chapter will compare and contrast Ghannouchi's, Qaradawi's, and Yassine's stance on reason versus faith, and democracy.

Chapter 5

1. People whose lineage goes back to the Prophet Muhammad.
2. *Islam or Deluge* 1974: 13.
3. Islam or Deluge1974: 20–21.
4. www.yassine.net—accessed October 24, 2010.
5. Also www.yassine.net—accessed October 24, 2010.
6. Yassine states that the "authorities" framed him for his earlier article in response to King Hassan (www.yassine.net accessed October 24, 2010).
7. www.yassine.net accessed October 24, 2010.
8. "We embark on research with the investigation of existing entities, scrutinizing the conditions of the things observed by the eye and the distinction of the particulars. Then, we investigate by means of perception the peculiarities of sight, what is constant and what is visible."

   He went on to say: "Then we advance, gradually and sequentially, in research and measurement while reviewing the premises and making reservations about the results. We make our investigation and scrutiny abides by the principles of objectivity, not biased judgment, and by the search for truth, not blind imitation of opinions ... Perhaps we shall finally attain by this method, based on gradual progress, careful criticism and making reservations, to the indisputable truth that removes all doubts" (Yassine 2003: 63).

9. "In its Western manifestation, modernity is reason's work itself, and hence above all of science, technology and education; the social politics of modernization should have no other goal than to disencumber reason's path by suppressing the rules, corporatist defenses, or customs barriers."

    "We are thus face to face with a modernity that eradicates, a modernist ideology which calls for 'disencumbering the way' so that 'enlightened humanity' might dispel the darkness of 'tradition'—a tradition which, in the eyes of the West, is currently incarnate in the 'illuminati' of an obscurantist Islam" (Yassine 2000: 3).

10. "Critical ideology, by far the most dangerous weapon of the lot, fires at everything that is ancient, decreeing it archaic, supported merely by the irrational, to be rejected as fraudulent because it claims its basis in some 'revelation' or 'superhuman' volition. Islam thus provides a direct target for modernism" (Yassine 2000: 7).

11. "Our kind of democracy is called *shura*. What wouldn't one do to make oneself understood by a French-speaker with no other point of reference than his Western culture, closed to every idea, every word that has other roots? What wouldn't one do to get one's meaning across to minds that are mystified and alienated by a secularist culture gulped down willingly or forcibly and assimilated to the point of becoming in itself the basis of some people's cultural metabolism?

12. As opposed to *'ibadat*: literally worship, i.e. the relationship between God and humans.

13. All those institutions are theological higher education institutions.

14. *Mu'tazalites* are a group of scholars who disputed certain religious issues. The literal translation of *Mu'tazilah* is seceders: "*Mu'tazilah*, in effect, was an umbrella term covering diverse scholars who were divided on a number of points but united on others" (Netton 1992: 185).

15. *Sira*: the sayings and deeds of the prophet.

16. The Companions thought if the prophet chose Abu Bakr to lead in prayer and issues that pertain to faith, shouldn't he also lead in daily life? Therefore, after discussion they offered him "*al-Bay'a*": the leadership of the Muslim *umma*.

Chapter 6

1. The textual sources are: the Qur'an and the Sunna (the deeds and sayings of the Prophet Mohammed).

2. Banna is the founder of the Muslim Brotherhood movement in Egypt in 1928. Banna did not believe in a multi-party system because to him this would have created divisions within the Muslim community. Those divisions would obstruct the unification of Muslims as indicated in the Textual sources.

3. "By attacking Christian political theology and denying its legitimacy, the new philosophy simultaneously challenged the basic principles on which authority had been justified in most societies in history. That was the decisive break. The ambition of the new philosophy was to develop habits of thinking and talking about politics exclusively in human terms, without appeal to divine revelation or cosmological speculation. The hope was to wean Western societies form all political theology and cross to the other shore....Our experiment continues, though with less awareness of why it was begun and the nature of the challenge it was intended to meet. Yet the challenge has never disappeared" (Lilla 2007: 5).

4. Timothy Lim writes: "Scholars and comparativists, so far, have been unsuccessful in developing a universal explanation about the process(es) of democratic transition and consolidation" (Lim 2006: 158).

5. Held writes: "Analysis of the variants of democracy, the chief task of this book, does not resolve them, although it may help to illuminate why certain positions are more attractive than others. In focusing on the chief variants, this volume will set out some of the political options we face today. But it is as well to say that these options do not present themselves in a simple, clear cut manner" (Held 2006: 3).

6. Shapiro expresses that: "People with insiders' wisdom in a given setting are more likely to know how to do this effectively. Solutions that they devise and embrace are more likely to command their allegiance than those imposed on them by outsiders" (Shapiro 2003: 147).

7. I use "political" Islam because most specialists refer to Islamic political activism as "political Islam". However, it is important to note that historically, since its inception, Islam was always political and social, i.e. there was no separation between the faith and all aspects of the social, political, and economic lives of its followers.

8. "In states with well-defined democratic processes, Islamists will likely conform to existing norms. In states with shaky democratic traditions and norms, the Islamists will be no more or less trustworthy as guardians of democratic process than most other parties" (Fuller 2003: 132-143).

9. Ernest Gellner identified himself as an "Enlightenment Rationalist Fundamentalist' as opposed to "Muslim Fundamentalists" (Gellner 1992).

10. Lilla adequately states: "Liberal theology began in rational hope, not fevered dreams. Its moderate wish was that the moral truths of biblical faith be intellectually reconciled with, and not just accommodated to, the realities of modern political life. Yet the liberal deity turned out to be a stillborn God" (Lilla 2007: 301).

11. Feldman writes: "The path of least resistance for Europe and the United States is to do nothing out of the ordinary, to wash their hands of the Muslim struggle against injustice while telling one another that national character is destiny, and that the Muslims have brought their troubles upon themselves. That distanced stance may salve the consciences of the former colonial powers of Europe and the American superpower today, but it must not be allowed to hide a tragedy for which the West is partly responsible. If nothing changes, to hide a tragedy for which the West is partly responsible (Feldman 2003: 197).

Bibliography

Abdel-Rahman, 'Umar. 1989: *Mithaq al-'Amal al-Islami (An Islamic Social Contract)*. Cairo: Maktabat Ibn Katheer.

Abou el Fadl, Khaled. 2004: *Islam and the Challenge of Democracy*. New Jersey: Princeton University Press.

Abu-Rabi', Ibrahim. 1996: *Intellectual Origins of Islamic Resurgence in the Modern Arab World*. Albany: State University of New York Press.

Apter, David. 1965: *The Politics of Modernization*. Chicago: University of Chicago Press.

Ayoob, Mohammed. 2008: *The Many Faces of Political Islam: Religion and Politics in the Muslim World*. Ann Arbor: University of Michigan Press.

Baker, Raymond W. 1990: *Sadat and After: Struggles for Egypt's Political Soul*. Cambridge: Harvard University Press.

Baker, Raymond W. 2003: *Islam Without Fear: Egypt and the New Islamists*. Cambridge: Harvard University Press.

Bayle, Pierre. 1740: *Dictionaire historique et critique*. Amsterdam: P. Brunel.

Binder, Leonard. 1971: *Crises and Sequences in Political Development*. New Jersey: Princeton University Press.

Burke, Edmund, and Ira Lapidus. 1988: *Islam, Politics, and Social Movements*. Berkeley: University of California Press.

Butterworth, Charles. 1982: *Islamic Resurgence in the Arab World*. (ed.) New York: Praeger Publishers.

Cesari, Jocelyne. 2004: *When Islam and Democracy Meet*. New York: Palgrave Macmillan.

Charnay, Jean-Paul. 1971: *Islamic Culture and Socio-Economic Change*. Leiden: E.J. Brill.

Cole, Juan. 2009: *Engaging the Muslim World*. New York: Palgrave Macmillan.

Cox, Caroline and John Marks. 2006: *The West, Islam and Islamism: Is ideological Islam compatible with liberal democracy?* London: Civitas: The Institute for the Study of Civil Society.

Dahl, Robert. 1956: *A Preface to Democratic Theory.* Chicago: The University of Chicago Press.

Darwish, Salih. 1992: *Hiwarat Rashid al Ghannouchi (A Collection of Interviews with Ghannouchi).* London: London: Khalil Media Service.

De Tocqueville, Alexis. 2003: *Democracy In America and Two Essays on America.* London: Penguin Books.

Deeb, Mary-Jane. 1992: *"Militant Islam and the Politics of Redemption".* The Annals of the American Academy of Political and Social Science 524.

Dekmejian, Richard. 1971: *Egypt Under Nasser.* Albany: State University of New York Press.

Dekmejian, Richard. 1985: *Islam in Revolution.* Syracuse: Syracuse University Press.

Esposito, John. 1988: *Islam: The Straight Path.* Oxford: Oxford University Press.

Esposito, John. 1992: *The Islamic Threat: Myth or Reality?* Oxford: Oxford University Press.

Esposito, John. 1997: *Political Islam: Revolution, Radicalism, or Reform?* Boulder: Lynne Rienner Publishers.

Esposito, John and Francois Burgat. 2003: *Modernizing Islam: Religion in the Public Sphere in Europe and the Middle East.* New Brunswick: Rutgers University Press.

Esposito, John and Azzam Tamimi. 2000: *Islam and Secularism in the Middle East.* New York: New York University Press.

Esposito, John and John Voll. 2001: *Makers of Contemporary Islam.* Oxford: Oxford University Press.

Euben, Roxanne. 1999: *Enemy in the Mirror: Islamic Fundamentalism and the Limits of Modern Rationalism.* New Jersey: Princeton University Press.

al-Fasi, Allal. 1972: *Difa'an 'an al-Shari'a (In Defense of Islamic Law).* Rabat: Manshurat al-'Asr al-Hadith.

Feldman, Noah. 2003: *After Jihad: America and the Struggle for Islamic Democracy.* New York: Farrar, Straus and Giroux.

Feldman, Noah. 2004: *What We Owe Iraq: War and the Ethics of Nation Building*. New Jersey: Princeton University Press.

Feldman, Noah. 2008: *The Fall and Rise of the Islamic State*. New Jersey: Princeton University Press.

Foucault, Michel. 1977: *Discipline and Punish: The Birth of the Prison*. New York: Vintage Books.

Fuller, Graham. 2003: *The Future of Political Islam*. New York: Palgrave Macmillan.

Gellner, Ernest. 1992: *Postmodernism, Reason and Religion*. London: Routledge.

Gerges, Fawaz. 1999: *America and Political Islam: Clash of Cultures or Clash of Interests?* Cambridge: Cambridge University Press.

Ghadbian, Najib. 1997: *Democratization and the Islamist Challenge in the Arab World*. Boulder: Westview Press.

Ghannouchi, Rashid. 1989: *Huquq al-Muwatana (Minority Rights in Muslim Societies)*. Herendon: International Institute of Islamic Thought.

Ghannouchi, Rashid. 1993: *Al-Huriyat al-'Aama fi al-Dawla al-Islamiya (Public Freedom in the Islamic State)*. Beirut: Markaz Dirasat al-Wihda al-'Arabiya (The Research Center of Arab Unity).

Ghannouchi, Rashid. 2001: *Min Tajrubat al-Haraka al-Islamiya fi Tunis (The Experience of the Islamic Movement in Tunisia)*. London: Maghreb Center for Research and Translation.

Ghannouchi, Rashid. Unpublished article (a): Is Secularism a Savage, or a Civilized and Free Philosophy?

Ghannouchi, Rashid. Unpublished article (b): Public Freedoms in Islam.

Ghannouchi, Rashid. Unpublished article (c): The Roots of Democracy and the Origins of Islamic Governance.

Glasse, Cyril. 1989: *The Concise Encyclopedia of Islam*. San Francisco: Harper Collins Publishers.

Gole, Nilufer. 1996: *The Forbidden Modern: Civilization and Veiling*. Ann Arbor: University of Michigan Press.

Gore, Al. 2007: *The Assault on Reason*. New York: The Penguin Press.

Habermas, Jurgen and Joseph Ratzinger. 2006: *Dialectics of Secularization: On Reason and Religion*. San Francisco: Ignatius Press.

Haddad, Yvonne. 1991: *The Contemporary Islamic Revival: A Critical Survey and Bibliography*. New York: Greenwood Press.

Hall, Cheryl. 2005: *The Trouble with Passion: Political Theory Beyond the Reign of Reason*. New York: Routledge.

Harris, Lee. 2007: *The Suicide of Reason: Radical Islam's Threat to the West*. New York: Basic Books.

Held, David. 2006: *Models of Democracy*. Stanford: Stanford University Press.

Hentsch, Thiery. 1992: *Imagining the Middle East*. Montreal: Black Rose Books.

Hoffman, Bruce. 1998: *Inside Terrorism*. New York: Columbia University Press.

Huntington, Samuel. 1991: *The Third Wave: Democratization in the Late Twentieth Century*. Norman: University of Oklahoma Press.

Huntington, Samuel. Summer 1993: *"A Clash of Civilizations?"* Foreign Affairs.

Huntington, Samuel. 1996: *The Clash of Civilizations and the Remaking of World Order*. New York: Simon and Schuster.

Kenz, Ali. 1991: *Algerian Reflections on Arab Crises*. Austin: Center for Middle Eastern Studies.

Kepel, Gilles. 1985: *The Prophet and the Pharaoh: Muslim Extremism in Egypt*. London: al-Saqi Books.

Kramer, Martin. 1997: *The Islamism Debate*. Tel Aviv: Tel Aviv University.

Lewis, Bernard. September, 1990: *"The Roots of Muslim Rage"*. Atlantic Monthly 266.

Lewis, Bernard. 2002: *What Went Wrong? Western Impact and Middle Eastern Response*. Oxford: Oxford University Press.

Lilla, Mark. 2007: *The Stillborn God: Religion, Politics, and the Modern West*. New York: Alfred Knopf.

Mabro, Judy. 1996: *Veiled Half-Truths: Western Travellers' Perceptions of Middle Eastern Women*. London: I.B. Tauris.

Miller, Judith. Spring 1993: *"The Challenge of Radical Islam"*. Foreign Affairs.

Moaddel, Mansoor and Kamran Talattof. 2000: *Modernist and Fundamentalist Debates in Islam*. New York: Palgrave Macmillan.

Al-Najjar, Abd al Majid. 2000: *The Viceregency of Man: Between Revelation and Reason*. Herndon: International Institute of Islamic Thought.

Netton, Ian. 1992: *A Popular Dictionary of Islam*. New Jersey: Humanities Press International Inc.

Noori, Ayatollah Yahya. 1987: *Legal and Political Structure of an Islamic State*. Glasgow: Royston Limited.

Parsons, Talcott. 1977: *The Evolution of Societies*. New Jersey: Prentice-Hall.

Al-Qaradawi, Yusif. 1973: *Shari'at al-Islam (Islamic Shari'a)*. Beirut: al-Maktab al-Islami.

Al-Qaradawi, Yusif. 1981: *Al Sahwah al Islamiyah bayn al-Juhud w'al-Tataruf (The Islamic Awakening between Rejection and Extermism)*. Qatar: Dar al-Ummah.

Al-Qaradawi, Yusif, 1994: *Fatawi Mu'asira (Contemporary Religious Opinions)*. Mansoura: Dar al-Wafaa Publishers.

Al-Qaradawi, Yusif. 1998: *Al-Sahwah al-Islamiya wa Humoom al-Watan al-'Arabi w'al-Islami (The Islamic Awakening and the Arab and Islamic Predicaments)*. Cairo: Dar el-Shorouk.

Al-Qaradawi, Yusif. 2000: *Priorities of the Islamic Movement in the Coming Phase*. Swansea: Awakening Publications.

Al-Qaradawi, Yusif. 2001 (a): *Min Ajl Sahwa Rashida (An Intelligent Awakening)*. Cairo: Dar el-Shourouk.

Al-Qaradawi, Yusif. 2001 (b): *Min Fiqh al-Dawla fi'l-Islam (Jurisprudential Insight into Running an Islamic State)*. Cairo: Dar el-Shorouk.

Al-Qaradawi, Yusif. 2001 (c): *Al-Sahwah al Islamiyah bayn al-Jumud w'al-Tataruf (The Islamic Awakening between Conservatism and Extremism)*. Cairo: Dar el-Shorouk.

Al-Qaradawi, Yusif. 2002: *Al-Sahwah al-Islamiya min al-Murahaqa illa al-Rushd (The Islamic Awakening from Adolescence to Maturity)*. Cairo: Dar el-Shorouk.

Al-Qaradawi, Yusif. 2002: *Al-Sira al-Dhatiya (Personal Autobiography)*. Cairo: Dar el-Shurouk.

Qutb, Sayyid. 1988: *Nahwa Mujtama' Islami (Towards an Islamic Society)*. Cairo: Dar al-Shuruq.

Rabinow, Paul. 1984: *Foucault Reader*. New York: Pantheon Books.

Rahnema, Ali. 2005: *Pioneers of Islamic Revival*. London: Zed Books.

Al-Raysouni, Ahmed. 1991: *Nazariyat al-Maqasid 'ind al-Imam al-Shatibi (The End Goals of Islamic Law According to al-Shatibi)*. Herendon: International Institute of Islamic Thought.

Said, Edward. 1978: *Orientalism*. New York: Vintage Books.

Said, Edward. 1993: *Culture and Imperialism*. New York: Alfred Knopf Inc.

Sardar, Ziauddin. 1985: *Islamic Futures: The Shape of Ideas to Come*. New York: Mansell Publishing Limited.

Schacht, Joseph. 1964: *An Introduction to Islamic Law*. Oxford: Oxford University Press.

Shapiro, Ian. 2003: *The State of Democratic Theory*. New Jersey: Princeton University Press.

Soroush, Abdolkarim. 2000: *Reason, Freedom, and Democracy in Islam*. Oxford: Oxford University Press.

Steet, Linda. 2000: *Veils and Daggers: A Century of National Geographic's Representation of the Arab World*. Philadelphia: Temple University Press.

Tamimi, Azzam. 2001: *Rachid Ghannouchi: A Democrat within Islamism*. Oxford: Oxford University Press.

Al-Turabi, Hassan. 1980: *Tajdid Usul al-Fiqh al-Islami (Renewing Islamic Jurisprudential Thought)* Beirut: Dar al-Jeel.

U.S.–Muslim Engagement Project. 2008: *Changing Course: A New Direction for U.S. Relations with the Muslim World*. Washington, D.C.

Vatikiotis, P.J. (ed.) 1981: *Islam and Power*. Baltimore: John Hopkins University Press.

Vidler, Alec. 1970: *A Variety of Catholic Modernists*. Cambridge: Cambridge University Press.

Wiarda, Howard. 2000: *Introduction to Comparative Politics: Concepts and Processes*. Orlando: Harcourt College Publishers.

Yassin, Abdel-Salam. 1994: *Al-Minhaj al-Nabawee (The Prophet's Ways)*. Beirut: Al-Sharika al-'Arabiya al-Ifriqiya l'il Nashr w'al-Tawzee'.

Yassin, Abdel-Salam. 1995: *Al-Islam w'al-Qawmiya al-'Ilmaniya (Islam and Secularism)*. Tanta: Dar al-Basheer.

Yassin, Abdel-Salam. 1996: *Al-Shoura w'al-Dimokratiya (Democracy and Consultation)*. Dar al-Baydha: Al-Ufuq.

Yassin, Abdel-Salam. 2000 I: *Al-'Adl (Justice)*. Dar al-Afaq.

Yassin, Abdel-Salam. 2000 II: *Al-Ihsan (Benevolence)*. Dar al-Afaq.

Yassin, Abdel-Salam. 2000 (a): *Winning the Modern World for Islam.* Iowa: Justice and Spirituality Publishing.

Yassin, Abdel-Salam. 2000 (b): *Al-Khilafa w'al-Mulk (The Caliphate and the Monarchy).* Dar al-Afaq.

Yassin, Abdel-Salam. 2003: *The Muslim Mind on Trial: Divine Revelation versus Secular Rationalism.* Iowa: Justice and Spirituality Publishing.

Yavuz, Hakan. 2003: *Islamic Political Identity in Turkey.* Oxford: Oxford University Press.

Suggested Reading

Abou El Fadl, Khaled. 2001: *Speaking in God's Name: Islamic Law, Authority and Women.*

Baker, Raymond. 2004: Islam *and the Challenge of Democracy.*

—— 2006: *Islam, the West and the Challenges of Modernity.*

—— The Great Theft. 2007: *Wrestling Islam from the Extremists.*

—— 2010: *Reasoning With God.*

Burgat, Francois. 1997: *The Islamic Movement in North Africa.*

—— *Modernizing Islam.* 2003: *Religion and the Public Sphere in the Middle East and Europe.*

—— 2004: *Face to Face with Political Islam.*

Esposito, John. 1999: *The Islamic Threat: Myth or Reality.*

Esposito, John. 2003: *Unholy War: Terror in the Name of Islam.*

—— 2010: *The Future of Islam.*

Feldman, Noah. 2004: *After Jihad. America and the Struggle for Islamic Democracy.*

—— 2008: The *Fall and Rise of the Islamic State.*

Glancy, Brian, 2007: *Liberalism Without Secularism? Rachid Ghannouchi and the Theory and Politics of Islamic Democracy.*

Ramadan, Tariq. 2008: Radical *Reform: Islamic Ethics and Liberation.*

—— 2009: Islam, *the West and the Challenges of Modernity.*

Shahin, Emad Eldin. 1998: *Political Ascent: Contemporary Islamic Movements In North Africa.*

—— 2004: *Contemporary Arab and Muslim Thought.*

—— 2009: *The Struggle Over Democracy in the Middle East.*

Skovgaard, Jakob, and Bettina Graf 2009: *The Global Mufti: The Phenomenon of Yusuf al-Qaradawi.*

Tamimi, Azzam, Rachid Ghannouchi. 2001: *A Democrat within Islamism.*

Voll, John, 1994: *Islam: Continuity and Change in the Modern World.*

—— and John Esposito. 2001: *Makers of Contemporary Islam.*

Index

Compiled by Sue Carlton

Page numbers in **bold** refer to definitions in the glossary. Page numbers followed by n refer to the endnotes.

Abdel Rahman, 'Umar 39
Abdel-Nasser, Gamal 19, 67, 68, 69, 86
Abdu, Muhammed 75, 77
Abou el-Fadl, Khaled 41–2
Abu Bakr 103, 104, 140n
Abul Magd, Kamal 59
Afghani, Jamal-al-Din 75, 77
Afghanistan, and al-Qaeda 6–8, 59, 113
al-Abbas, Al-Hajj 89
Al-Jama'a al-Islamiya 91
al-Jama'a magazine 91
al-Sabah (The Morning) (periodical) 90
al-Albani, Sheikh Nasser al-Din 70
Andalusia 32–3, 95
Arab unity 68, 69
atheism 12, 90
  atheist rationalism 93, 96, 97, 98, 99, 105, 113
  see also secularism/ secularization

Ba'athism 69
Baker, Raymond W. 54–5, 56–7, 107

al-Banna, Hassan 8, 44, 46–8, 60, 112, 134n, 141n
Batchouchiya Zawiya (Sufi order) 89, 105
al-Bayani, Abu Abdallah 40
Bayle, Pierre 12
Ben Ali, Zine El Abidine 75
Bennabi, Malik 75, 76, 81–2
Bergson, Henri 13, 118
Berque, Jacques 17, 27
bin Laden, Osama 6–7
Bourguiba, Habib 68, 69, 72, 75
Burke, Edmund 18
Burton, Sir Richard 15–16
Butterworth, Charles 4

Catholic Church 51
charismatic authority 18–19
Charnay, Jean-Paul 29–30
Chateaubriand, François-René de 16
Christianity 11–12, 13, 78, 87, 108, 116, 141n
  and democracy 25
civilizational Islam 59
clash of civilizations 8, 24, 123
Cold War paradigm, inadequacy of 6–7

colonialism/colonization 14–17, 96

common good 38, 90, 120

Darwin, Charles 14
Davis, Winston 17, 133n
da'wa 46, 71, 72, 89, **128**, 136n
Deeb, Mary-Jane 18
dehumanization of 6, 15–16
  see also Orientalism
deists 12, **126**
Dekmejian, Richard 18–19
democracy/democratization 11, 18, 19, 24–5, 26, 27, 41, 119–25
  and Christianity 25
  Ghannouchi on 80–3, 87, 112–13, 124
  political Islam and 122–5
  Qaradawi on 43, 60–4, 112, 113, 124
  and secularism 5, 97, 98, 114, 119–20, 140n
  Yassine on 96–9, 106, 113, 124
  see also shura
Descartes, René 12
dhaniyat 36, 63, 79, **128**
Durkheim, Emile 118

Egypt 8, 14, 19, 46, 47, 68–9, 87
  see also Abdel-Nasser, Gamal; Nasserism
Emara, Mohammed 10

Enlightenment 10–14, 19–21, 26–7, 51, 78–9, 114–20, 124–5
  and colonialism 14, 15
  fixation 3–4
  Ghannouchi on 80–1, 82, 87, 108
  Yassine on 94–5, 96–7, 106
  see also rationality/reason
Enlightenment Rationalist Fundamentalist 1, 11, 142n
Esposito, John 4, 5, 9, 27, 31, 37, 41–2, 122
Euben, Roxanne 2–4, 20–1, 27–8, 118, 119, 132n
extremists/extremism 57, 58, 62, 111
  see also fundamentalism

al-Farabi, Mohamed 34
al-Fasi, Allal 31
Feldman, Noah 9, 122, 124, 142n
Fernea, Elizabeth 25
fiqh (Islamic jurisprudence) 2, 30–2, 35, 38, 57, 95, **128**, 133n, 138n
  fiqh al-muwazana 58, 135n
  fiqh al-Sunan 56, 135n
  fiqh of balance 43, 56
  fiqh of the end goals of Sharia 43, 56, 57
  fiqh of priorities 43, 56
  fuqaha 36, 37, 38, **128**
  Usul al-Fiqh 36, 40, 41, **131**
fitra 89, **128–9**

Foucault, Michel 10, 11, 21, 23,
    114, 119, **126**, 133n
freedom 15, 78–9, 83–6, 87, 111
    democracy and 61, 82, 84, 87,
        97, 98
    of expression 85–6, 98, 99,
        121
    of thought 86, 96
Freud, Sigmund 13
fundamentalism 3, 20–1, 27,
    132n

Gellner, Ernest 1–2, 10–11,
    19–20, 132n
Geraudy, Roger 75
Gerges, Fawaz 10
al-Ghannouchi, Rachid 9, 32,
    38, 66–87, 107–13, 122,
    136–9n
    on democracy 80–3, 87,
        112–13, 124
    exile in London 76
    on *ijtihad* and *tajdid* 66,
        79–80, 87, 109–10
    imprisonment 74–5
    and MTI 71–6
    on public freedom 78–9, 82,
        83–6, 87, 111
    on reason and faith 76–9,
        80–1, 82, 87, 108, 117
al-Ghazali, Al-Sheikh 48
Gole, Nilufer 25–6
Granada 32–4
green peril 8

Habermas, Jurgen 118, 119
Haddad, Yvonne 4, 5

hadith 38, **129**, 133n
Hall, Cheryl 116, 119
Hanafi, Hassan 10
Harris, Lee 123–4
Hassan, King of Morocco 88,
    89–90, 101, 105, 139n
Hegel, G.W.F. 15
Held, David 120–1, 141n
Hentsch, Thierry 14, 15, 17
humanism 114
Huntington, Samuel 8, 24–5, 27,
    123, 124

Ibn al-'Aas, 'Amr 59, 138n
Ibn al-Haitham 95, 108
Ibn al-Khattab, 'Umar 84, 102
Ibn al-Nafis 46
Ibn al-Qayim 70
Ibn Asim, Abu Yehya 40
Ibn Khaldoun 76
Ibn Lobb, Abu Said 36
Ibn Rushd 46, 95
Ibn Sina 95
Ibn Taymiya 70
Al-Ifadat wa al-Inshadat
    (Shatibi) 35
ijma' 36, 37, 101, **129**
ijtihad 5, 37, 41–2, 109–11,
    129, 135n, 136n, 137–8n
    Ghannouchi on 66, 79–80,
        87, 109–10
    Qaradawi on 53, 55–7, 59,
        65, 109–10
    versus *taqlid* 109–10
    Yassine on 100–1, 106, 109,
        110
Inchbold, A.C. 16

Iran 62, 112–13
Iranian Revolution (1979) 1,
        5–6, 22, 73, 74, 112, 124
irrationalism 13
al-Isfahani, Dawud ibn Khalaf
        (al-Zahiri) 135n
Islam
    and God's rules 32, 103
        see also sharia
Islamic law 5, 28, 34–5, 36, 55,
        63–4
        *see also fiqh; maqasid;
        maslaha; sharia*
Islamic Legal Studies Program
        (Qatar University) 50
Islamic movements 3, 8, 19, 23,
        26–8, 109–10, 122–4
    see also Islamists
Islamic state 4–5, 9, 39, 62, 65,
        99, 106, 122
Islamic Tendency Movement
        (MTI) (*later al-Nahda*)
        71–6
    imprisonment of members
        74–5
Islamic trend 69, 70, 86
Islamists 22, 34, 53–4, 60
    moderate/liberal 1, 6, 9–10,
        37, 42, 111, 114, 117, 119,
        122, 132n
    populist 7–9
    see also Islamic movements;
        political Islam
istihsan 35, 37, **129**
istikhlaf 85, **129**, 137n
istishab 38–9, **129**
istislah 37, **129**

Al-Itisam (Shatibi) 34–5, 36

al Jazeera 51, 55
Justice and Benevolence
        movement (Morocco) 88,
        91, 92, 105

al-Kady, Abu Bakr 40
Kant, Immanuel 11–12, 94,
        127–8
Karl, Terry Lynn 121
al-Kawakibi, Abdul Rahman 77
Kenz, Ali 18
Kepel, Gilles 23
Khalil, Naseef 46
Khilafah (guardianship) 101–4,
        106, **129**
Khomeini, Ayatollah 73
al-Khuli, Bahi 44–5
kingship 101–4, 105
Kitab al-Majlis (Shatibi) 35
Kramer, Martin 122–4

Lamartine, Alphonse de 16, 27
Lane, Edward 16
Lebonne, Gustave 54
Lewis, Bernard 10, 24, 27
Lilla, Mark 115–17, 119, 124,
        141n, 142n
Loftus, William Kennett 16

Maghreb 69, 70, **129**
Manzoor, Ahmed 31
al-maqasid (end goals of *sharia*)
        34, 36–9, **130**, 133n
    Qaradawi on 38, 43, 56,
        57–8, 64, 65

Shatibi on 34, 36, 82, 86
Yassine on 100–1, 106
Marshall Plan 22
Mashreq 69, 70, **129**
maslaha (public welfare) 36–9,
    42, 58, **130**, 133n, 135n
  Ghannouchi on 85, 86
  Qaradawi on 37–8, 57, 62, 64
  Shatibi on 35, 36, 40, 82, 86
  Turabi on 39
  Yassine on 90, 101
Massignon, Louis 17
Miller, Judith 24
modernity/modernization 21–6,
    61, 78, 93, 100, 133n
  Islamic law and 34, 39
  and rationality 1, 11, 17–18,
    96, 97, 140n
  and secularism 20, 114,
    116–17
  and Western standards 10
Muhammad, Prophet 103
Muhammad VI, King of
    Morocco 88, 92, 101
mujtahids 55–6, 100–1, **130**
Muslim Brotherhood 8, 9, 45–9,
    50, 69, 72, 91, 105
  dissolution of 47–9
  imprisonment of Brothers
    48–9
Mu'tazalites 101, 110, **130**,
    140n
Al-Muwafaqat (Shatibi) 34,
    36–9

al-Nadawi, Sheikh Abu
    al-Hassan 50

al-Nahda (Renaissance Party)
    32, 38, 66, 75, 76
  see also Islamic Tendency
    Movement
al-nass 36, 64, **130**
Nasserism 67, 69, 70, 86, 105
NATO 22
Nazism 13
Nietzsche, Friedrich 13, 118
Noori, Ayatollah Yahya 30–1

Orientalism 16–17, 27, 53–4,
    95, 101
Other, the 4, 14, 15–16, 99
Ottaway, Marina 121
Ottoman Empire 14–15, 77

pan-Arabism 67, 68, 69–70, 86,
    105
Pareto, Vilfredo 118
Pipes, Daniel 124
Piscatori, James 22–3
Plato 115
political Islam 7, 8, 9, 142n
  and democratization 122–5
  see also Islamists

al-Qaeda 6–7
al-Qaradawi, Yusuf 9, 37–8,
    43–65, 107–13, 122, 134n
  on *al-wasatiya* (centrality) 43,
    58–60, 64, 65, 111
  and democracy 43, 60–4, 112,
    113, 124
  and *ijtihad* and *tajdid* 53,
    55–8, 59, 65, 109–10
  imprisonment 48–9

al-Qaradawi, Yusuf *continued*
  and media 51, 54–5
  and Muslim Brotherhood 45,
    46–9, 50
  on reason and faith 52–5,
    107–8, 117
qat'iyat 36, 39, 63, **130**
al-qiyas 35, 36, 37, **130**, 135n
Qur'an 52, 53, 54, 57, 78, 79,
    91, 92–3
  and Islamic law 29, 32, 36,
    37, 38, 133n, 135n
Qutb, Sayid 32, 62, 72, 112

Rabinow, Paul 114
rasonieren 11, **127–8**
Ratzinger, Joseph (Pope Benedict
    XVI) 118–19
al-Razi, Fakhr 46
reason/rationality 11–14, 17–21,
    123–4
  and faith 5, 27, 34, 107–9,
    114–19, 124
    Ghannouchi on 76–9, 80–1,
      82, 87, 108, 117
    Qaradawi on 45–6, 52–5,
      64, 107–8, 117
    Shatibi on 34, 41
    Yassine on 92–6, 105–6,
      107–8, 117
  see also rasonieren
Rousseau, Jean-Jacques 98,
    115–16, 117, 119

Sadat, Anwar, assassination of
    22
Said, Edward 16–17, 27, 123

Sardar, Ziauddin 37
Saudi Arabia 7
Schacht, Joseph 30
Schmitter, Philippe C. 121
Schopenhauer, Arthur 13
secularism/secularization 2, 29,
    61, 69, 96
  and democracy 5, 97, 98, 114,
    119–20, 140n
  and modernity 20, 114,
    116–17
September 11, 2001 terrorist
    attacks (9/11) 1, 6, 8
Shahin, Emad 91, 122
Shapiro, Ian 120, 141n
al-Sha'rawi, Al-Sheikh 45, 134n
sharia 2, 29–32, 34, 36–7, 60,
    62, **130**
  and democracy 63–4
  fiqh of the end goals of 43, 56,
    57
  see also al-maqasid
al-Shatibi, Abu-Ishaq 9, 28,
    32–42, 82, 86, 133n, 138n
shura 41, 60, 61, 86, 96–9, 100,
    135n
  and democracy 96–9, 106,
    113, 140n
sira 103, **130**, 140n
Sorel, George 13, 118
Soviet Union (USSR) 22
Spencer, Herbert 14
Steet, Linda 25
Structural Functionalism 21–2,
    26
Sudan 73–4

sunna 57, 78, 79, 100, **131**,
  135n
  and Islamic law 29, 32, 36,
    37, 135n, 238
  'Sunna and Sira' Research
    Center 50–1
Syria 70–1

tabligh 71–2, 136n
al-Tahtawi, Rifa'a 77
tajdid 55–6, 79, 99, 100, **131**,
  137n
Taliban 59
Tamimi, Azzam 9, 72, 73, 77,
  79–80, 82, 136–8n
taqlid 79, 109, 137n
Tehran hostage crisis 5, 7
theocracy 62
Tocqueville, Alexis de 116,
  117–18, 119
traditionalism 18, 30, 93
truth 4, 12, 21, 52, 93, 139n,
  142n
Tunisia 66–8, 71–6, 136n, 137n
al-Tunsi, Khayr el-Din 75, 77
Al-Turabi, Hassan 32, 38–9

Umma 47, 52, 61, 82–3, **131**
United States (US) 6, 7, 22
Usul al-Fiqh 36, 40, 41, **131**

Vatikiotis, P.J. 23
Voll, John 9, 27, 122
Voltaire 12

Wasat Party (Egypt) 59
al-wasat/wasatiya (centrality) 43,
  58–60, 64, 65, 107, 111, **131**
Weber, Max 17–19, 21–2, 114
women
  in MTI 73–4
  Muslim 15–16
  in Muslim societies 25–6, 40

Yassine, Abdessalam 9, 88–106,
  122, 139–40n
  on guardianship and kingship
    88, 101–4, 105, 111
  on *ijtihad* 100–1, 106, 109,
    110
  imprisonment 88, 89, 91
  letters to King 88, 89–90, 92
  on reason and faith 92–6,
    105–6, 107–8, 117
  on *shura* and democracy
    96–9, 106, 113, 124
  under house arrest 88, 90, 92
Yassine, Nadia 88
Yavuz, Hakan 9

al-Zaytouna, 68–9, 101, 136n